QUIT SMOKING BOOT CAMP

QUIT SMOKING BOOT CAMP

THE FAST TRACK TO QUITTING SMOKING AGAIN... FOR GOOD

To Joyce Carr & Madi Lewis

and to

*Tim Glynne-Jones & Nigel Matheson for their
amazing contribution in making this book happen*

This edition published in 2018 by Arcturus Publishing Limited
26/27 Bickels Yard, 151–153 Bermondsey Street,
London SE1 3HA, UK

AD005772UK

Printed in the UK

ALLEN CARR

Allen Carr was a chain-smoker for over 30 years. In 1983, after countless failed attempts to quit, he went from 60–100 cigarettes a day to zero without suffering withdrawal pangs, without using willpower, and without putting on weight. He realized that he had discovered what the world had been waiting for, the easy way to stop smoking, and embarked on a mission to help cure the world's smokers.

As a result of the phenomenal success of his method, he gained an international reputation as the world's leading expert on stopping smoking and his network of centres now spans the globe. His first book, *Allen Carr's Easy Way to Stop Smoking*, has sold over 12 million copies, remains a global bestseller, and has been published in more than 40 different languages. Hundreds of thousands of smokers have successfully quit at Allen Carr's Easyway centres where, with a success rate of over 90 per cent, they guarantee you'll find it easy to stop or your money back.

Allen Carr's Easyway method has been successfully applied to a host of issues including weight control, alcohol, debt, and other addictions. A list of Allen Carr centres appears at the back of this book. Should you require any assistance or if you have any questions, please do not hesitate to contact your nearest centre.

For more information about Allen Carr's Easyway, please visit **www.allencarr.com**

Allen Carr's Easyway

The key that will set you free

CONTENTS

INTRODUCTION

Do you find there's never enough time for all the things you need to do in life? Are you putting off your attempt to quit smoking until you can find the time to commit to it properly? If so, this is the book for you. You don't have to wait for the right time; you can enlist for the Easyway Boot Camp right now and begin your mission to quit smoking immediately.

Four days from now, you will be a happy non-smoker. Do you find that hard to believe? Well, I have only good news for you, read on...

We hear it all the time: "There are never enough hours in the day." If only you could quit smoking or vaping quickly, painlessly and permanently, think of the energy, money, and time you would have to spend on things you genuinely enjoy. But quitting smoking is not something that just happens overnight, right? Some people take months or even years and still don't seem to be completely rid of their desire to smoke. Who's got the time for all that!

That was my attitude to smoking before I finally quit. "Sure, quitting would be nice but I don't have the time right now." I led a busy life, I had a successful career, and dealing with the pressures that brings – I relied on cigarettes for my little crumbs of comfort. Of course, they weren't really giving me comfort; they were only adding to my stress. But I was too wrapped up in my perception of life and the huge role that smoking played in it to see the truth. I needed someone to hold it up in front of my face.

I was very fortunate. Somebody did hold the truth up for me to see. Twenty or so years ago, I attended Allen Carr's clinic in London to see if he could help me quit my 80-a-day smoking addiction. I attended under duress. I had agreed to go, at the request of my wife, on the understanding that when I walked out of the clinic still a confirmed smoker she would leave it at least 12 months before hassling me about stopping again. No one was more surprised than me, or perhaps my wife, that Allen Carr's Easyway method set me free.

If I had been more open-minded, it would not have surprised me. By the time I went along Allen had already helped millions of people to quit through his clinics and books. The evidence was plain to see but, being a chain-smoker whose entire existence revolved around "the next cigarette", the worst nicotine addict I knew, I couldn't see it. In hindsight, I can say that part of me didn't want to see it. It took my own personal life-changing experience to convince me.

For a third of a century, Allen had chain-smoked 60 to 100 cigarettes a day. With the exception of acupuncture, he'd tried all the conventional and unconventional methods to quit without success. Eventually he gave up even trying to quit, believing: once a smoker, always a smoker. Then he discovered something that motivated him to try again.

As he describes it, "I went overnight from 100 cigarettes a day to zero – without any bad temper or sense of loss, void or depression. On the contrary, I actually enjoyed the process. I knew I was already a non-smoker even before I had extinguished my final cigarette and I've never had the slightest urge to smoke since."

It was a revelation to Allen – who immediately realized that he had discovered a method of quitting that would enable any smoker to quit:

Easily, immediately and painlessly

Without using willpower, aids, substitutes or gimmicks

Without suffering depression or withdrawal symptoms

Without gaining weight

After using his smoking friends and relatives as guinea pigs, he gave up his lucrative profession as a qualified accountant and set up a clinic to help other smokers to quit. He called his method EASYWAY, and so successful has it been that there are now Allen Carr's Easyway centres in more than 150 cities in 50 countries worldwide. Bestselling books based on his method are now translated into over 40 languages, with more being added each year.

It quickly became clear to Allen that his method could be applied to any drug. The method has now helped tens of millions of people to quit smoking, alcohol, illicit drugs, and to deal with sugar addiction, over-eating, and fear of flying, as well as to stop gambling and overspending.

I was so inspired by Allen and what I saw as his miraculous method that I hassled and harangued him and Robin Hayley (now chairman of Allen Carr's Easyway) to let me get involved in their quest to cure the world of smoking. To my good fortune, I succeeded in convincing them. Being trained by Allen and Robin was one of the most rewarding experiences of my life. To be able to count Allen as not only my coach and mentor but also my friend was an amazing honour and privilege.

Over the past 20 years, I have gone on to treat more than 30,000 smokers myself at Allen's original London clinic and lead the team that has taken his method from Berlin to Bogota, New Zealand to New York, Sydney to Santiago. Tasked by Allen with ensuring that his legacy achieves its full potential, we've taken Allen Carr's Easyway from videos to DVD, from clinics to apps, from computer games to audio books, to online programs, video-on-demand and beyond.

Behind this phenomenal success lies one simple truth – a truth that Allen discovered by chance and passed on to tens of millions of people like me. What connects us all is that none of us expected to be changed in the way we were. We were all sceptical, all labouring under the same illusions. There is a vast army of smokers and vapers out there still suffering their own private nightmare, believing that they enjoy smoking or vaping, that it provides them with some kind of benefit, and that as a result, it's hard to quit.

The truth about smoking is kept hidden from most smokers and even from many ex-smokers. That's why some who quit using willpower continue to crave cigarettes long after they stub out their final cigarette. They believe they are making a sacrifice, resigned to doing without something that provides them with pleasure or support, believing that it helps them to control their weight, to relax, to socialize, and to handle stress. Understanding the simple truth and recognizing how it applies to you is the key to escaping the nicotine trap and staying free permanently. But it takes a special method to do that.

ALLEN CARR'S EASYWAY IS THE METHOD THAT WORKS

This book, like all Easyway books, will help you to see the simple truth. It is designed to help busy smokers, coping with the demands of 21st-century life, with no time to waste, smokers who appreciate clear no-nonsense guidance and who like to feel they're getting the job done as they go along. It doesn't rely on guilt, bullying, fear, or scare tactics; as you will learn, all those techniques actually make it harder to quit. Easyway Boot Camp gives you a structured, easy-to-follow method for quitting quickly, painlessly and permanently.

I remember Allen telling me about his time as a Royal Air Force Drill Instructor during his national service – but don't worry – if you're imagining the Easyway Boot Camp in those kind of terms, think again. There are no tough drills, no one's barking orders at you, and no scare or shock tactics are involved; the clue is in the name "Easyway".

The Easyway Boot Camp simply divides the method into four days: on Day One you will develop a true understanding of smoking and how it holds you and millions of other smokers in its grip; on Day Two you begin to unravel the myths and illusions that keep you trapped; Day Three is your day of decisive action, when you deal a fatal blow to your addiction; and by the end of Day Four you are ready to enjoy life as a happy non-smoker. If you're someone who vapes, or uses 'snus' or 'dip' or any other nicotine product, as I've alluded to already, this book will work for you (even if you smoke AND vape). For the most part, this book will refer to smoking but virtually every aspect can be related to the use of all nicotine products.

Easyway Boot Camp is designed to get the job done. In under a week, you will go from committed smoker or nicotine addict to happy non-smoker and non-addict. Any scepticism you feel now will be gone, replaced by a complete, liberating understanding of nicotine addiction and a wonderful absence of any desire to ever smoke again, vape, or use nicotine in any form again.

The responsibility for ensuring our books are faithful to Allen Carr's original method is mine. It's been suggested to me that I describe myself as the author of the books we've published since Allen passed away. In my view that would be quite wrong.

That's because every new book is written strictly in accordance with Allen Carr's brilliant Easyway method. In our new books, we have merely updated and amended the format to bring it up to date and make it relevant for all those who wish to free themselves from addiction today. For example, we now need to provide guidance regarding the use of e-cigarettes or the ingesting of nicotine in any form other than by cigarette, cigar, or pipe.

In doing this, Allen Carr's Easyway organization is continuing its mission; to carry on Allen's amazing quest to cure the world of smoking and to apply his method to assist anyone suffering from any addiction or issue to which it can be applied.

There's not a word in our books that Allen didn't write or wouldn't have written if he was still with us today and, for that reason, the updates, anecdotes and analogies that are not his own work – that were contemporized or added by me – are written clearly in Allen's voice to seamlessly complement the original text and method.

I consider myself privileged to have worked intimately with Allen on Easyway books while he was alive, gaining insight into how the method could be applied to every conceivable addiction or issue. Together, we explored and mapped out the future evolution of the method. I was more than happy to have the responsibility for continuing this vital mission placed on my shoulders by Allen himself. It's a responsibility I accepted with humility and one I take extremely seriously.

In truth, I didn't know anything about addiction before I had the good fortune to meet Allen Carr. Not only did he free me from an addiction that would otherwise have killed me a long time ago, but he taught me everything I know about curing addiction: how it works, and how the Easyway method can tackle it, enabling anyone to quit smoking easily, painlessly and without the need for willpower.

Having worked on Allen's books for nearly 20 years, I still take pleasure in deflecting all the praise and acclaim straight back to the great man himself: it's all down to Allen Carr.

The method is as pure, as bright, as adaptable and as effective as it's ever been, allowing us to apply it to a whole host of addictions and issues aside from smoking. Whether it's alcohol or sugar addiction, gambling or junk spending, or fear of flying, mindfulness or even "hard drugs", the method guides those who need help in a simple, relatable, plain-speaking way. I know from happy experience that the benefits of following this method can be life-changing. Graduation from Allen Carr's Easyway Boot Camp, your freedom, is just four days away! And now let me pass you into the safest of hands – Allen Carr.

John Dicey

Global CEO & Senior Therapist, Allen Carr's Easyway

DAY ONE

GET TO KNOW YOUR ENEMY

I was the worst smoker on the planet. Smokers are notorious for burying their head in the sand. You can only continue to do something that you know is harmful and degrading if you close your mind to the fact. As a result, nicotine addiction becomes a lonely experience. Ironically for something that is supposed to be a sociable activity, it leaves smokers and vapers feeling like they have a problem that is unique to them.

But I can tell you now:

YOU ARE NOT ALONE

As you read this book, thousands of other smokers are doing the same thing – trying to find a cure to their smoking problem.

You *have* taken the crucial first step of opening your mind to the fact that you want to stop smoking. You have admitted that there is something about smoking or nicotine use that makes you unhappy – you may not know exactly what it is yet, but you know it's serious and you want to find a solution.

So, think of yourself as part of a big group, all with the same problem, all desperate to escape the tyranny of nicotine addiction. Welcome to the Easyway Boot Camp.

Some people spend their lives trying and failing to quit smoking. Others quit in an instant. If you think that's because there are different types of smoker, think again.

All smokers are caught up in the same trap. I tried and failed on numerous occasions before I discovered the method that enabled me to quit permanently.

What changed? It was my understanding of the problem.

Like most smokers, I believed that cigarettes gave me some sort of pleasure or crutch. I believed this, even though I took no pleasure in smoking and it made me feel miserable. I didn't realize that I was being fooled; that I'd simply fallen into the most sinister and subtle trap that man and nature have ever combined to devise. A mixture of brainwashing and addiction had led me to believe that smoking provided me with something beneficial or pleasurable.

As soon as I saw through the illusion, my desire to smoke disappeared and I was able to help other nicotine addicts quit easily, immediately and painlessly, without relying on willpower or substitutes, or having to endure any unpleasant withdrawal feelings. I'm going to spend "Day One" of this Easyway Bootcamp looking at your understanding of smoking and why you think you do it. By the end of the day you will have developed a real understanding of why you smoke, why you've been unable to quit until now, how smoking distorts and disrupts your behaviour, and what action you need to take to begin your successful bid for freedom.

Before you put this book down for the night, you will have laid the groundwork for "Day Two" and "Day Three", when you begin in earnest the simple task of freeing yourself from your slavery to nicotine. By the end of Day Four you will be free.

All you have to do is follow the instructions.

There is no need to stop smoking or vaping or using any other nicotine product or to try to change your smoking pattern until you reach the end of the book. In fact, it's important that you keep smoking or vaping as usual. Don't worry that the idea of carrying on smoking for the time being makes you happy and don't be concerned if the idea of quitting on "Day Four" makes you feel nervous or anxious or miserable. Trust that this book will answer every single question and any doubt that you might have. We have four days to lead you to a new life as a happy non-smoker.

Right now, you are still a smoker, so if you feel the urge to smoke a cigarette, go ahead. It's important that you don't do anything that you might consider to be depriving yourself. I will explain why later on. Likewise, if you haven't smoked for more than a day or so, but remain hooked on e-cigarettes, nicotine gum or patches or any other nicotine product, carry on using that product as you have done until now – without attempting to cut down or control your use.

For now, all you need to know is that this Boot Camp is not about pain – there is no pain when you quit with Easyway. You don't need willpower; you just need to follow the instructions. In four days, you will be free from smoking. Follow the instructions and you will discover how easy it is to get free from nicotine and, more importantly, stay free.

Now, if you're ready, let's get started.

WHY DO YOU SMOKE?

SMOKERS GIVE ALL SORTS OF REASONS WHEN ASKED WHY THEY SMOKE. THEY SELDOM GIVE THE CORRECT ANSWER. SO, WE ARE GOING TO BEGIN BY MAKING SURE YOU'RE AWARE OF THE REAL REASON YOU SMOKE.

INTRODUCTION TO NICOTINE

When you smoke a cigarette, you inhale a drug called nicotine. You could replace the word drug with poison. Let's strip it down and examine it.

In its pure form, nicotine is a colourless, oily compound that is lethal to humans in relatively small doses. It is the fastest-acting addictive drug known to mankind, faster than heroin. Each puff on a cigarette delivers a dose of nicotine to the brain, via the lungs, within just seven seconds – that's faster than a dose of heroin injected directly into the bloodstream.

If you take 20 puffs to smoke a cigarette, then you're taking 20 doses with every cigarette you smoke… this is like "machine-gunning" nicotine into your body.

Nicotine is quick to enter the system but it is also quick to leave it too. As soon as you stub out a cigarette, the nicotine level rapidly subsides and the drug begins to withdraw from your body. If you measured the amount of the drug in your bloodstream after smoking a cigarette, you would find it had fallen to roughly half after 30 minutes and to about a quarter after an hour. This explains why the standard pack contains 20 cigarettes and most smokers average a pack a day. After one hour, the withdrawal triggers the need for another. If you're like I was as a smoker, puffing your way through three or four packs a day, don't worry, it doesn't mean that you're more addicted, and it doesn't mean that you'll find it harder to quit.

WHAT DO YOU UNDERSTAND BY WITHDRAWAL?

Most smokers associate the word with the "terrible pangs and cravings" they suffer when they try to quit. In fact, the physical symptoms of withdrawal are so slight as to be almost imperceptible. Don't misunderstand me: the unpleasant physical symptoms you suffered when you may have attempted to quit previously are real; they're just not caused by nicotine withdrawal; they're a physical response to a mental process, of "wanting a cigarette" but not being able to have one.

I'll explain more later, but if, just on principle, you can accept that, then you have taken a huge step towards being free already. If you're not sure you can accept that, even in principle, don't panic; let's look at it in more detail.

THE UNPLEASANT PHYSICAL FEELINGS ARE REAL, BUT THEY
ARE THE RESULT OF A MENTAL PROCESS – OF WANTING
A CIGARETTE AND NOT BEING ABLE TO HAVE ONE

Think of a child having their favourite toy taken away from them; the physical symptoms it causes are real and measurable: red face, bulging eyes, anger, rage, an anxious, uptight and insecure feeling.

Does that sound familiar? Doesn't it describe the feeling you've had in the past when you've tried to quit smoking without success? But the fact is, the child isn't suffering from the physical withdrawal from a drug; it's simply a selection of physical symptoms, resulting from a mental process, "I WANT IT! I CAN'T HAVE IT! AGHHHH!"

It's "wanting a cigarette or an e-cigarette" that causes the really unpleasant symptoms when you try to break free from nicotine addiction rather than it simply being the physical withdrawal from nicotine:

"I WANT A CIGARETTE! I CAN'T HAVE ONE! AGHHHH!"

The physical response to that thought process is that uptight, anxious, churned-up, angry feeling that you identify as physical withdrawal.

The only reason you "want a cigarette" is because you believe it will do something positive for you.

Therefore, if I can explain that smoking, or nicotine in any form, does absolutely nothing for you, and furthermore if I can explain how you got fooled into thinking that it did in the first place, then you won't want a cigarette. True?

So let's take it a stage further. If you don't want a cigarette, then you won't have that "I WANT A CIGARETTE! I CAN'T HAVE ONE! AGHHHH!" feeling.

That's a lot to take in, especially so early on in this process, but please read the text from "What do you understand by withdrawal?" again, just to recap on this point. I don't want you to agree entirely with what I'm saying at this stage. I just want you to consider the possibility that what I am saying is true; to at least have an understanding of where I'm coming from.

NO WILLPOWER REQUIRED

Any real discomfort smokers experience when they try to quit is mostly mental as they wrestle with the thought of wanting something they can't have and feel the need to battle the temptation to smoke again.

Doesn't this make sense of those ex-smokers you meet from time to time – the ones who haven't smoked for months or even years but are still tearing their hair out? They don't have a trace of nicotine left in their body – so there is no physical withdrawal at all – yet they still mope after the drug. It's the "moping" that causes the unpleasant physical feelings, not nicotine withdrawal.

But you won't go through this discomfort. With Easyway, there is no mental struggle. That's why you don't need willpower.

The physical withdrawal from nicotine is so slight most smokers aren't even aware that they suffer it every day, and every night, of their smoking lives. Most of them are never aware of it. It manifests itself as nothing more than a mild, empty, slightly insecure feeling – not unlike hunger – which you interpret as the feeling of "something's missing".

Nicotine is an addictive drug that hooks you very quickly – just one cigarette is enough – but luckily, it's just as easy to get "unhooked". Nicotine leaves your system completely within a few days. Why, then, do smokers find it so hard to quit? And why do smokers who have not smoked for months or even years still crave a cigarette?

THE ADDICTION IS 1% PHYSICAL AND 99% MENTAL!

Given that is true, can you see how pointless it is to use nicotine products in an attempt to quit being addicted?

E-cigarettes, nicotine patches and gum, nicotine inhalators and lozenges attempt to address just 1% of the problem, leaving you suffering the other 99% – the mental side. No wonder you've failed in the past. Handle the mental side of things and the 1% physical addiction is easy to break.

When I first started helping smokers to escape from the smoking trap, it was actually quite difficult to have them understand that they were addicted.

These are more enlightened times and most smokers and vapers these days are fairly comfortable with the idea that they're addicts.

The issue that remains though is the belief that to be addicted to something you have to enjoy it, or get pleasure from it, or get some form of benefit from it.

By the time you graduate from the Easyway Boot Camp, you'll have a clear understanding of how addiction *really* works. And trust me, it has nothing to do with "liking" the drug, "enjoying" the drug, or getting "pleasure" or "benefits" from the drug.

If you began this book unaware that you're addicted, or reluctant to accept that you are, you will end the day fully accepting that you are addicted to nicotine and that that puts you in the same situation as someone who is addicted to heroin or any other drug.

This can be hard for nicotine addicts to accept. Smoking is a much more socially acceptable drug than heroin and most smokers prefer to think of it as "just a habit" they fell into and can't seem to kick, rather than seeing themselves as drug addicts. But the acceptance that you're addicted to nicotine is key to your escape. Seeing yourself as anything but a drug addict will lead to misconceptions about why you smoke and what smoking does for you, and it's these misconceptions that keep smokers in the trap.

Only by recognizing that you are an addict can you begin the process of becoming a non-addict again.

An addictive drug like nicotine works in a fiendishly clever way. Within seven seconds of lighting a cigarette, a fresh dose of nicotine is supplied to the brain and the slightly edgy feeling of withdrawal from the previous cigarette subsides. This creates the impression of satisfaction, relaxation and confidence, which smokers naturally attribute to the cigarette.

Think about that for a moment. Every single time you've lit a cigarette, every single day of your life as a smoker, you've felt slightly better than the moment before. But all that happened, on every single occasion, is the cigarette momentarily got rid of the unpleasant feeling caused by the previous one. This is the very slight, very mild, feeling of nicotine withdrawal. It's so slight you've been unaware of it for most of your smoking life.

In fact, if you were to pay attention to the cigarette and the way you feel as you prepare to light it (very few, if any, smokers do this), you would notice that the edgy feeling ends as soon as you take the cigarette from the packet and bring it to your lips. It doesn't take seven seconds. You don't even need to light it. You don't need the drug to relieve the withdrawal symptoms; you just need to know that you're about to get it. This goes to show that addiction is not a condition of the body but mainly of the mind.

ADDICTION IS 1% PHYSICAL AND 99% MENTAL

It's your mind that we are working on today, making sure you're fully prepared to accept the changes that will lead you to freedom from smoking, freedom from addiction.

When we first start smoking we're not aware of this process of withdrawal and relief because the pangs are so slight that we don't notice them. As smoking becomes a regular part of our life we assume it's because we enjoy it or we've just got into the "habit". It doesn't cross our minds that we've become addicted. But when you understand how addiction works, it's easy to accept that you are addicted to nicotine, and that addiction is not driven by genuine pleasure or genuine relief, it's a simple confidence trick.

Imagine someone you think of as a friend, without your knowledge, stealing $100 (or £100) from your bank account. After doing so, imagine they give you $10 (or £10) to spend on whatever you want. It would appear to be a lovely thing for them to do. They'd appear to be generous and kind. But are they really?

Is the $10 real? Of course it is. How can you view someone giving you $10 as being anything other than kind and generous? It's only when you have all the information, only when you find out that the $10 was already yours and, more than that, the thief has kept another $90 of yours in their back pocket, that you see the 'gift' of $10, and the so-called friend, as they really are. A sham. A con. A rip-off!

If you're thinking, "Well, at least they gave $10 of the $100 back to me – they could have taken it all," remember, this thief has been stealing from you like this for years. He doesn't deserve one ounce of gratitude.

THE LITTLE MONSTER

The first cigarette introduces nicotine into your system for the first time. You stub it out and for the first time you experience the physical withdrawal from nicotine. It's as if the first cigarette created a little nicotine monster inside your body, like a tapeworm, that feeds on nicotine.

As the nicotine withdraws from your body, the little nicotine monster expresses its dissatisfaction. It's a mild, empty, insecure feeling, so slight it's almost imperceptible. When you light your next cigarette, the mild, empty, slightly insecure feeling disappears (you've effectively fed the little monster) and you feel slightly better than a moment before. A lifetime's chain has started.

Whatever you may think are your reasons for continuing to smoke, there is only one reason: to feed the Little Monster.

You know what it's like when a neighbour's burglar alarm has been ringing all day? You find a way to blot it out so you can get on with other things, but then suddenly the alarm stops and you experience a wonderful sense of relief. The peace feels heavenly, but all you're enjoying is the end of the aggravation. It's the same when a smoker lights a cigarette and feeds the Little Monster. All you're trying to do is get rid of the aggravation of nicotine withdrawal. It's an empty, insecure feeling that is hard to pinpoint but nevertheless leaves you feeling slightly out of sorts.

Non-smokers don't suffer with that feeling and neither did you before you started smoking. So why do you smoke?

TO FEEL LIKE A NON-SMOKER

Many smokers will argue until they're blue in the face that smoking gives them pleasure. But the only pleasure you can hope to get from smoking is the feeling of removing the aggravation caused by the Little Monster and restoring the state of calm and confidence that you had before you became addicted. In fact, you can never return to the state of calm and confidence of a non-smoker by smoking.

THE ONLY WAY TO FEEL LIKE A NON-SMOKER IS BY NOT SMOKING

The great news is that the Little Monster is actually very weak – it's easy to kill. What the Little Monster does though is act as a trigger for the Big Monster, a mental process that develops as a result of you appearing to feel better after lighting each cigarette. The effect of this process, day in, day out, every single day of your smoking life confuses your brain into thinking that the cigarette provides some kind of pleasure or crutch. It's like being fooled by the conman who steals $100 from your bank account without your knowledge and then gifts you $10.

Before you started smoking your body was complete. Then you forced nicotine into your body and as the drug started to leave, your body suffered the slightly restless feeling of withdrawal. It wasn't a physical pain; in fact, it was so slight you probably didn't consciously register it. Your reaction to it, though, was to light another cigarette.

Time passes by and your conscious mind doesn't understand the feelings or your response to them. All you know is that you want another cigarette, and when you have one the slightly empty feeling goes. Again, you don't really register the feeling going, you just feel a little better, a little more confident and complete than a moment before. In fact, the way you felt was how you felt your whole life before you first smoked. It was nothing more than relieving the aggravation caused by the first cigarette.

And so it goes on, each cigarette creating the desire for the next. It's a vicious circle that ties you up for life – unless you break the cycle.

Exercise: **PAY ATTENTION**

Smokers say they enjoy smoking. They insist that they like the taste, the smell, the feeling of the cigarette in their hand. In truth, the vast majority of cigarettes are smoked without you being aware of the taste, smell, feel or any other aspect of what you're doing.

When you smoke your next cigarette or e-cigarette, pay attention to every part of the process. Concentrate on the packet or device – how does it look? What do the cigarettes look like in there? What does the cigarette look and feel like as you take it out of the packet? And how do you feel?

Hold the cigarette under your nose and take notice of how you feel as you sniff the tobacco. How is your heartbeat?

Continue applying this level of attention as you go through your usual routine, placing the cigarette between your lips, lighting it, inhaling that first drag of smoke, blowing the smoke away from your face and eyes. As the cigarette burns down, how does it smell? How does it taste? What is the sensation on your tongue? In your throat? In your nose? In your lungs? How does the cigarette look between your fingers? As you reach the end and crush it out, how does it look in the ashtray? What taste has it left in your mouth? And how do you feel inside?

I'm not expecting this exercise to put you off smoking. That is not the point. What is important is that you have a clear perception of the truth when it comes to your personal experience of smoking. At the moment, your perception of smoking is shrouded in a fog of brainwashing. Like all smokers, you assume there must be something marvellous about the cigarette that keeps you coming back for more.

> Make no mistake, the only reason you come back for more is to feed the Little Monster.
>
> Please be vigilant here; if you are a smoker please smoke a cigarette as I described above, completing the exercise before you move on. Likewise, if you vape or use dip, or any nicotine product or device, adapt the exercise accordingly. Only then are you ready to move on. Don't feel under any pressure to draw any conclusions from the exercise – however you feel is perfectly fine.

A LOGICAL CONCLUSION

If smoking is just an addiction, then it follows that you don't do it for pleasure or a crutch, to help you concentrate or feel more confident. Does a heroin addict inject the drug because it helps him concentrate? Of course not. It's easy to see that a heroin addict continues to take the drug because the addiction makes him feel terrible when he has to go without. There is nothing more complex or sophisticated about it than that. Be careful not to fall for Hollywood's glamorized view of drugs as being the providers of an amazing high. For the most part, someone taking heroin for the first time doesn't feel fabulous or high or amazing; in fact, it's quite the reverse.

So it should be just as easy to see smoking in the same light. You smoke to get nicotine. You only want nicotine because you're addicted to it – the Little Monster makes you feel restless and empty without it.

And if addiction to nicotine is the only reason smokers smoke, or vapers vape, or dippers dip, then it doesn't make any difference who the smoker is. There is no genetic difference between smokers and non-smokers and there is no difference between different types of smoker. Smoking is simply a trap into which anybody can fall if they light an experimental cigarette. Because once you've put nicotine in your body, all it takes is the second cigarette to feed the Little Monster and you begin a lifetime's journey into the nicotine pit.

THIS IS GREAT NEWS.

If the only reason you smoke is because you're addicted to nicotine, all you need to do to quit is remove the addiction. You don't have to "give up" anything; there is no sacrifice, no deprivation. You don't need to draw on all your reserves of willpower to resist the temptation to smoke because there is no temptation. Neither is there anything in your personality to hold you back. All there is is a gradual descent into addiction, which, you'll be delighted to know, is easy to reverse.

BREAK THE CHAIN AND YOU WILL BE FREE.

The real trick, and the one essential to making it easy to not just stop, but to stay stopped – and not just to be a non-smoker, but to be a happy non-smoker – is to truly understand why you thought you got tremendous pleasure, enjoyment and support from taking this drug.

We've dealt with the principle and process of the addiction, the Little Monster; later we'll deal with the brainwashing, the Big Monster. It's the Big Monster that has caused the torture and hell, along with the feelings of deprivation in your previous attempts to quit.

BRAINWASHING

Despite the success of Easyway, smoking remains the world's number one killer. Working against us is a hugely powerful machine that continues to brainwash people into believing that they choose to smoke because it gives them some sort of pleasure or crutch.

I don't just mean the tobacco industry. Television and movies continue to play an influential role in portraying smoking as something cool, suave and characterful. Every celebrity seen with a cigarette in their mouth is responsible for hundreds if not thousands of impressionable fans taking up smoking.

Against this weight of propaganda, how is any smoker expected to see the simple truth?

YOU DO NOT CHOOSE TO SMOKE

Think about it – if you had any choice over whether you smoke or not, you wouldn't be reading this book. You smoke because you are caught in a trap and because if you've tried to quit in the past, you've failed to do so. This time it's going to be different.

Smokers who cannot see and understand this simple truth find it hard to quit. Why? Because they go about it in the wrong way. Follow the right method and quitting is easy. The starting point is understanding why you smoke.

THE NICOTINE TRAP

WE'VE ESTABLISHED THE REAL REASON WHY YOU SMOKE – BECAUSE YOU'RE IN A TRAP CALLED NICOTINE ADDICTION. NOW WE NEED TO EXAMINE THE TRAP YOU'RE IN, LEARN HOW IT WORKS AND UNDERSTAND HOW YOU CAN ESCAPE.

THE PITCHER PLANT

The more subtle a trap is, the more effective it is at catching unsuspecting victims. The nicotine trap is so ingenious that not only do its victims not see it coming, they don't even realize when they've been caught. It only dawns on them when they're well and truly hooked and struggling to escape.

A good comparison is the pitcher plant, that carnivorous wonder of nature that feeds on flies. The pitcher plant is so-called because of its distinctive jug shape. The plant's nectar attracts flies, which alight on the upper rim of the pitcher and start to feed. The fly has no fear of the plant. Why should it? It can fly off whenever it wants. But right now the nectar tastes good, so there's no reason to think about flying away.

As the fly continues to feed, it ventures deeper into the pitcher. The sides are steeper here and slippery with sweet nectar. The fly loses its grip occasionally and turns back towards the light, but the nectar is too good to resist and the instinct to fly away is not triggered until it's too late. By the time the fly realizes that there's something wrong about this plant, it's lost its grip and fallen into the digestive juices at the bottom of the pitcher. Now it's the plant devouring the fly, rather than the other way around.

With the nicotine trap, there is no sweet nectar to lure victims in. The lure is purely psychological. We all light our first experimental cigarette for a variety of foolish reasons. From birth we're brainwashed into believing that it might help us to fit in, to appear more grown up, to seem more sophisticated, or to be rebellious. The list is endless. First-time smokers find the taste and smell revolting, yet they are still drawn into the trap because somewhere in their mind the seed has been sown that smoking is something that can give them pleasure. They're not exactly sure what that pleasure is – and those first puffs certainly don't offer any insight – but they know enough people who do it to convince them that it's worth the effort.

The revolting taste and smell of cigarettes is enough to prevent some first-time smokers from ever smoking a second time, and thus never getting hooked, but for others it contributes to the deadly lure of the trap.

It makes them think, "I could never get hooked on this", and so they stumble on, confident that they could stop any time they choose. Like the fly, their confidence is dreadfully misplaced.

SECURITY OF THE PRISON

The nicotine trap is not just ingenious in the way it snares its victims. Even when they realize they're hooked and desperately wish they could escape, the trap grips them tighter, making the idea of escape seem more daunting than the prospect of staying in the trap.

There is a similar psychological effect with long-term convicts when they're finally released from prison. Rather than embracing their newfound freedom, a large proportion of prisoners reoffend within a short period of their release. They don't do it because they believe that crime will pay and they'll get away with it this time; they do it because they want to get caught and put back inside. They crave what they've come to consider the security of the prison.

Prison may be tough, confined and miserable but for the long-term convict it offers the comfort of familiarity. The world outside is daunting and full of questions: Can I fend for myself? How do things work? Will I cope with all the changes? Will anyone want to know me? For smokers, the nicotine trap offers the same feeling of "security". This is what grips you and makes it hard to escape. You know that smoking is deadly, that it's already damaging your health and wealth, yet the prospect of living life without cigarettes, suffering torture and hell in the attempt to get free, and the assumption that, even if you succeed in quitting, you'll end up feeling miserable and deprived for the rest of your life puts you off the idea of even trying to quit.

Rather than seeing the nicotine trap as a hellish prison that they want to escape from at the earliest possible opportunity, smokers feel a sense of being trapped between a rock and a hard place.

THE TUG-OF-WAR OF FEAR

The force that drives the long-term prisoner to reoffend so soon after being released is FEAR. Smokers block their minds to the devastating effects of smoking for the same reason. If they paid heed to what they know to be the truth about smoking, they would have to stop – and that frightens them even more. This explains why smokers spend their lives blocking their minds to the many powerful reasons to quit and search for any flimsy excuse to have "just one more" cigarette.

Smokers are pulled apart by a constant tug-of-war that takes place in their mind. On one side is the voice saying, "It's killing me and costing me a fortune. It's filthy, disgusting and it's controlling my whole life."

On the other is a voice saying, "How can I enjoy life and cope with stress without my little pleasure or crutch? Quitting won't be easy. Do I have the willpower to even try? And will I ever be able to say I'm completely free?"

There is one thing at both ends of this tug-of-war: FEAR. It is overwhelmingly fear that keeps smokers trapped. At one end the fear of what will happen to us if we carry on smoking – on the other side, the fear of what will happen if we stop; how will we cope?

This Easyway Boot Camp will get rid of both of those fears. Don't worry, I have no intention whatsoever of preaching to you about the downsides of smoking. You know all about those already. The biggest mistake that government health campaigns make is to utilize fear to encourage smokers to stop.

Firstly, as smokers we turn a blind eye to it anyway. The moment someone on the radio or TV starts talking about the damage caused by smoking we simply switch channels. Even on those rare occasions that we allow ourselves to dwell on the downsides of smoking, in situations where we're forced to do so, what's the first thing we do? We light a cigarette. A smoker's reaction to any stressful situation is to light a cigarette. Attempting to cure a smoker by telling them about the damage it's causing to them is not only an insult to their intelligence, but a complete waste of time; it's entirely counterproductive, like trying to extinguish a fire with a bucket of petrol.

As soon as you're a happy non-smoker, the fear of being a smoker disappears. It's a fabulous feeling of freedom. One you can anticipate with relish. Getting rid of the fear on either side of the tug-of-war, the worry about how you'll cope without cigarettes, how you'll handle stress, how you'll manage to relax, control your weight, enjoy socializing, and live everyday life without cigarettes is what this Boot Camp will achieve.

THE PLEASURE OF SMOKING

As I demonstrated in the last exercise, most smoking is done without paying any attention. The only times you're aware of it are when you're coughing and wheezing and wishing you'd never started; or when you're breathing smoke into the face of a non-smoker and feeling embarrassed and anti-social; or when you're running out of cigarettes and beginning to panic; or when you're in a situation where you're not permitted to smoke and you're feeling deprived.

So what sort of pleasure is that? A "pleasure" that, when you're doing it, you're either not aware that you're doing it or you're wishing you weren't, and that only seems precious when you can't do it! Yet smokers are terrified by the prospect of spending the rest of their life without it.

THE BIG MONSTER

The lure of the nicotine trap is purely psychological. Nobody takes up smoking because they are drawn to the taste or smell. It's the belief that they are getting into something a bit naughty or pleasurable, or beneficial, that lures them in.

It's the same belief that keeps them trapped. The smoker's tug-of-war of fear exists because of the belief that smoking gives you some sort of pleasure or crutch. Take away that belief and the arguments for smoking simply disappear. Smoking becomes exposed for what it really is: pointless. And if there is genuinely no point in doing something, why would it require any willpower not to do it? It doesn't. You'll no more be inclined to stick a cigarette in your mouth than you might be to stick it in your ear.

I've introduced you to the Little Monster, which feeds on the nicotine from each cigarette and complains as the nicotine leaves your system. When you smoke the next cigarette, the Little Monster is satisfied and you feel a sense of relief flooding back in. But then it floods back out and the Little Monster starts moaning again. This is the cycle of addiction. Smokers believe that cigarettes relieve their stress and help them relax and concentrate. They don't realize that it's smoking that causes these problems in the first place.

KILL THE LITTLE MONSTER AND YOU END THE ADDICTION

All you have to do to kill the Little Monster is starve it of nicotine – it dies within a matter of days. That's how long it takes for the physical traces of nicotine to leave your system; in fact most of it leaves within 24 hours, and any withdrawal pangs are so slight you'll barely be aware of them.

So why has it been so hard to quit until now?

Millions of smokers have tried to quit with willpower alone or willpower combined with nicotine patches or gum or e-cigarettes. Yet they have found that they still craved a cigarette weeks, months, even years after the Little Monster had died. They have applied all their willpower to resist the cravings, but it only takes one offer of a cigarette at a party, or in some stressful situation like a road accident or hospital emergency, or something as simple as a bust-up with their partner, and the trap door opens up and drags them in once again.

The fact is, if quitting was as straightforward as stopping smoking and waiting for the Little Monster to die, everybody would do it without fail. But there is a second monster, as I've mentioned already, the Big Monster that lives in the mind, and it's this that keeps smokers craving cigarettes long after they've quit.

The Big Monster is your perception of smoking as a pleasure or crutch. It is created by all the brainwashing from the tobacco industry, the entertainment world, other role models and even anti-smoking campaigners, who persist in giving smokers advice that is almost guaranteed to keep them smoking, rather than helping them to quit. These well-meaning but ill-informed folk perpetuate the myth that smoking is a habit, a pleasure, a crutch; that smokers smoke because they choose to; that smokers enjoy smoking; and – the greatest myth of all – that smoking is hard to stop.

When the Little Monster starts craving nicotine, the minute physical feeling is enough to awake the Big Monster. Without the influence of the Big Monster, it would be easy to dismiss the cries of the Little Monster and carry on with your life without smoking, but the Big Monster interprets that faint, empty feeling as "I want a cigarette" and convinces you that the only way to relieve the craving is to smoke or vape.

This is the ingenuity of the nicotine trap. Each cigarette causes the craving for the next. And the belief that smoking gives you pleasure or a crutch is reinforced by the feeling of relief as one cigarette, or e-cigarette, fills the emptiness left behind by the previous one.

YOUR OBJECTIVE

By now you should be beginning to understand why it's so important to prepare your mindset before we move on to the next stages of helping you to quit nicotine. Your mind is currently occupied by a Big Monster that keeps convincing you that the drug is the solution to all your insecurities and discomforts. You believe it because every time you smoke you feel a sense of relief and interpret this as pleasure. But the "pleasure" is nothing more than the partial relief of the discomfort caused as you experience withdrawal from the previous cigarette. In other words,

THE ONLY PLEASURE FROM SMOKING OR VAPING IS THE PARTIAL RELIEF OF THE DISCOMFORT CAUSED BY SMOKING OR VAPING

It's like wearing tight shoes all day just for the relief of taking them off. Why subject yourself to the pain in the first place?

When a smoker begins to understand how the nicotine trap works, you can see a light click on in their eyes. It's a revelation. Most smokers go through life not even aware that they're in a trap. They think they smoke because they choose to (although they can't understand why), or because it helps them to relax (even though it actually makes them more stressed), or helps them to concentrate (even though it's a constant distraction).

Until the nicotine trap is explained, smokers and vapers are left with a headful of contradictions that tug them in opposite directions: the tug-of-war of fear. "I know it's killing me" versus "how can I go through life without it?" The solution is easy:

KILL THE BIG MONSTER

In order to do that, we need to unravel all the brainwashing that gave birth to the Big Monster in the first place.

ESCAPE IS EASY

A smoker is like a fly in a pitcher plant, but there is one crucial difference. By the time the fly realizes it's in danger, the opportunity for escape has passed. The smoker, on the other hand, can escape at any time. The ingenuity of the nicotine trap is also its weakness. You have the power to escape any time you choose because…

YOU ARE YOUR OWN JAILER

Nobody is holding a gun to your head and forcing you to smoke. Addiction is what keeps you trapped. Once you've realized this simple fact, you can cure the addiction and walk free any time you want.

Here's a prediction. In just four days you will be a happy non-smoker. You will have walked out of the nicotine trap and you will have found the process incredibly easy. Perhaps you find that hard to believe right now.

That's OK. You're not going to be required to do anything hard. In fact, I'm going to make life as easy for you as possible by setting out some simple instructions.

All you have to do is follow the instructions and you can't fail to quit smoking easily, painlessly and permanently.

FIRST INSTRUCTION: FOLLOW ALL THE INSTRUCTIONS

Four days is no time to spend on something as life-changing as quitting smoking, yet you may well be feeling impatient already. Perhaps you're champing at the bit already, wanting to get on with it, or perhaps it's the complete reverse – you're thinking about bailing out on the idea because it all seems too good to be true.

If you're in the former category, keep your discipline; don't be tempted to skip ahead and miss out parts of the programme. If you're in the latter group, understand one thing: nothing bad is going to happen in four days. You're either going to find it easy to stop or not. If you fail, you'll be no worse off than you are now. You really have nothing to lose, so if for no reason other than curiosity, or even simply to prove me wrong, just carry on reading while you carry on smoking, and follow the instructions.

We need to make sure that all the brainwashing is unravelled and that the Big Monster is well and truly dead when you come to smoke your final cigarette or have your final dose of nicotine. We can only achieve that if you follow all the instructions. It's like the combination to unlock a safe. I could give you all the numbers for the combination, but if you left any out or didn't put them in the right order, the safe would remain tight shut.

The only exception to this instruction is this: in the event that you wish to complete this Easyway Boot Camp in three, or two, or even one day rather than four, then you should feel free to do so. As long as you read the book in its entirety, and follow all the intructions, you will succeed.

THE MYTH

YOU SHOULD NOW UNDERSTAND THAT THE REAL REASON YOU SMOKE IS PURELY TO SATISFY THE LITTLE MONSTER THAT YOU CREATED WHEN YOU SMOKED YOUR FIRST CIGARETTE AND THE ONLY REASON YOU BELIEVE THAT SMOKING WILL RELIEVE YOUR CRAVING IS BECAUSE OF A BIG MONSTER IN YOUR MIND THAT INTERPRETS THE CRIES OF THE LITTLE MONSTER AS "I WANT A CIGARETTE". THE NEXT STEP IS TO RECOGNIZE THAT YOU HAVE BEEN BRAINWASHED.

WE'VE ALL BEEN BRAINWASHED

Smokers and non-smokers are brainwashed into believing a myth. The brainwashing is relentless and all of us are exposed to it from the day we are born. It comes in many forms and from many sources and you rarely hear it challenged. The net result of all the brainwashing is the myth that smoking offers some sort of pleasure or crutch.

The brainwashing is so all-consuming that even non-smokers believe it. Most people who have never smoked, or been inclined to smoke, will believe there may be something relaxing or stress-relieving in smoking. You can't really blame them; their attitude is often one of incredulity: "There's no way that smokers would suffer all the dangers and disadvantages of smoking if they didn't get something from it."

Even smokers who appear to smoke for pure pleasure give away their true feelings. I'm talking about those smokers who only smoke a few cigarettes a day. The implication is that they are in control, choosing where and when they smoke, unlike chain-smokers who light up one cigarette as soon as they stub out the last.

But those casual smokers are caught in exactly the same trap and they know it. They love to tell you that they can go days without a cigarette if they have to. Now why would they do that if they thought smoking was a genuine pleasure or crutch?

A lot of people love exercising. You never hear them bragging about how long they can go without exercising.

They would exercise all the time if they could because they love it and it makes them feel good. For them, exercising is a genuine pleasure. Smokers are always trying to fight the urge to smoke. What kind of a pleasure is that?

As long as you continue to perceive smoking as a pleasure or crutch, you will always find it hard to quit. But as soon as you can see that any perception of pleasure or crutch is an illusion created by a combination of brainwashing and addiction, you will find it easy and enjoyable to quit.

THE DELUSION OF ENJOYMENT

We all know the pitfalls of smoking. The health risks are drummed into us from a young age along with all the brainwashing but, rather than putting us off ever trying a cigarette, the negative publicity adds to the myth. The element of danger, the taboo, the rebellion... this is what attracts us to smoking that first cigarette. It has nothing to do with how the cigarette actually tastes or smells.

But ask a youngster why they've started to smoke and they'll tell you they enjoy it. That's strange, because they don't look like they're enjoying it as they cough and splutter and try not to wretch if they accidentally take the smoke down into their lungs.

Ask them again after a few weeks, when they're inhaling like an old-timer, and they'll tell you they enjoy the taste and smell. They're not making it up this time. They actually believe that they have acquired the taste for it. In reality, they've just got used to the vile taste, smell and effect on their lungs.

Just a few weeks later they'll answer the same question by saying smoking relaxes them, helps them concentrate and gives them confidence. In a very short time, their perception of smoking has evolved from something that tasted and smelt disgusting into something that tastes good, smells good and offers them a crutch. The myth is cemented in their mind and they're proud to be seen as a smoker.

But it doesn't stay this way. Ask them again after a few years and they're more likely to answer defensively that it's just a habit they got into. This answer betrays the shame and helplessness they feel. They know there's nothing good about smoking now, nothing to be proud of. It's become a major drain on their finances and they're becoming aware of the impact on their health and relationships, yet they've also found themselves powerless to stop doing it. Whenever they summon up the willpower to attempt to quit, they feel deprived and miserable and return to smoking.

If the fly could see it was in a trap before it started to slide down the pitcher plant, it would fly away. You have that chance. Take it!

The excuses for smoking keep changing but the real reason never does. Despite reaching the stage where it's obvious that smoking is giving you no pleasure or crutch, you keep smoking to try and end the empty, insecure feeling that the first cigarette created. But each cigarette does not end that feeling, it does the very opposite.

EACH CIGARETTE REKINDLES THE CRAVING AND ENSURES THAT YOU SUFFER IT OVER AND OVER FOR THE REST OF YOUR LIFE

The only way to stop the craving is to stop feeding the Little Monster. Very soon it will die and the physical discomfort will stop. There are two ways to kill the Little Monster: the hard way and Easyway. Kill the Big Monster first and quitting is easy.

YOUR SURVIVAL TOOLKIT

Think back to that first ever cigarette you smoked. All your instincts will have been telling you to avoid it, yet something in your mind made you persevere. If you had listened to your instincts, you would not be in this predicament now.

The human body is an incredible machine. Its powers of recovery are extraordinary. We abuse our bodies with all sorts of poisons – nicotine, alcohol, sugar, etc. – yet our bodies keep soldiering on, and any time you decide to stop abusing yourself and lead a healthier lifestyle, your body recovers with extraordinary speed. It's not just your body that feels healthier either. Your mind responds to the way you live too. Eat healthily, take exercise and you feel better mentally as well as physically. The reverse is also true: abuse your body and your mental health suffers too.

You have been equipped with a remarkable natural toolkit for survival. It consists of a number of reflexes, such as fear, pain, fatigue, etc., which all serve to help keep you alive. Ironically, we tend to regard these things as weaknesses. Without them, we would not last very long.

For example, we tend to equate fear with cowardice, but without fear you would wander blindly into deadly dangers, such as fire, heights and water. Fear is an instinct designed to help us avoid danger. When threatened, our fear sends us into survival mode: fight, flight or freeze. Without it, our ancestors wouldn't have survived.

Smokers often complain that they suffer with nerves and need cigarettes to calm them. Beside the fact that smoking will only make their nervous state worse, they're overlooking the fact that nerves are part of the survival toolkit. If you jump out of your skin every time a door slams, that's the same instinctive response as the one that sends the birds flying from the trees at the sound of a gunshot. OK, so you may feel you overreact to sudden noises. When you've quit smoking, you will find your nerves are a lot less frayed.

Fatigue and pain are other instincts we try to fight off with caffeine drinks and painkillers. We ignore the warning signs. Fatigue is your body's way of telling you that you need rest. Pain is your body's way of telling you it's being attacked and you need to tackle the cause, not keep trying to suppress the symptoms with drugs.

By tackling the symptoms rather than the cause, as so much of modern medicine does, we don't just allow the cause to continue, meaning the pain will get steadily worse; we also develop a tolerance against the drugs, meaning we need bigger and bigger doses to get the same effect. It's the same downward spiral that occurs with any drug, including nicotine.

Your senses are a vital part of your survival toolkit and when you smoked that first ever cigarette, your senses of taste and smell would have been screaming at you to stop. They would have detected poison and the strong revulsion you felt would have been their signals telling you "DON'T TOUCH!"

We share these survival tools with the rest of the animal kingdom, yet while all other animals heed the warnings, we choose to override them. Why do you think that is?

WHO'S GIVING THE ORDERS?

The tool that distinguishes human beings from the rest of the animal kingdom is intellect. It is another wonderful tool. Our intellect enables us to make judgements based not only on what is happening in the here and now but also on past experiences and even the experiences of others. It also helps us to predict future outcomes by using our imagination and projecting our experience on to hypothetical situations.

Thanks to this incredible tool, we have created sophisticated civilizations with remarkable architecture, art, literature, music, philosophy, sport and science. We no longer need to hunt for food, gather our own fuel for warmth or fight off predators. We have been able to share our intellect with future generations, ensuring the constant progression of technology and ideas.

But our intellect has also led us into disaster. Wars, weapons, drugs, slavery, prejudice and murder are all products of human intellect. But this hasn't dampened our pride in our intellect, nor our faith in the power of human reason. And so, when our intellect and our instincts conflict, it's our intellect from which we take orders.

The problem begins at birth, when the shock of coming into the world leaves us clinging to our mothers for security. In childhood, our parents comfort us with fairy tales and other make-believe: the tooth fairy, the Easter bunny, Santa Claus…

Then comes the day when we discover that none of this fantasy world exists. Our view of our parents changes. It begins to dawn on us that they are not the towers of strength we thought they were; they're fallible, and they have weaknesses and fears just like we do.

The disillusionment leaves a void, an empty, insecure feeling, which we instinctively want to fill. We begin to let other people into our lives to fill the void and with them come other influences. We look to people who appear to have the confidence we crave: rock stars, movie stars, sports stars, TV celebrities, models. These people become our role models and we copy their behaviour in the hope that it will lead us to be more like them – or the way we perceive them, anyway. If they dye their hair, we dye our hair. If they go to clubs, we go to clubs. If they drink, we drink. If they smoke, we smoke.

Instead of becoming complete, strong, secure and unique individuals in our own right, we become impressionable fans, leaving ourselves wide open to suggestion. But we don't want our insecurities to show; we want to look self-assured, confident, in control, grown-up. So we begin to mimic the mannerisms of other apparently confident individuals. We think they look cool when they smoke and drink and we know smoking and drinking are "grown-up" things to do because that's what the law suggests and that's what we've always been told.

And so we see smoking as a fast track to adulthood. Everything we have ever been told, including the warnings, leaves us in no doubt that smoking is a rite of passage.

The desire for security is instinctive. The belief that smoking provides security is intellectual. It's a myth that has been put in your mind by a lifetime of brainwashing. As humans, our incredible ability to communicate and absorb information is matched by our ability to communicate and absorb misinformation.

When you come to smoke that first ever cigarette, your instincts do everything in their power to stop you. Your senses of taste and smell scream "POISON! DON'T TOUCH!!"

If you persist, other reflexes kick in. You cough and may even vomit as your body tries to eject the poison. Carry on regardless and another sophisticated process goes into action: you build a tolerance to the poison, so your senses no longer react so violently against the taste and smell. What smokers believe to be an acquired taste is, in fact, an acquired lack of taste, as you knock out your natural warning system.

You put yourself through this trauma because you believe the prize will be worth it. You've been brainwashed into believing that cool confidence awaits you. By the time you think you've acquired the taste, you're already well and truly hooked and the cycle of addiction is drawing you deeper and deeper into the trap. All that awaits you is the miserable life of a smoker.

DISTINGUISHING INSTINCT FROM INTELLECT

If you trusted your instincts over your intellect, you would never have smoked that first cigarette. Like so many of the human race, you didn't, but it's never too late to learn.

As I pointed out earlier on, most cigarettes are smoked without the smoker paying any attention to it whatsoever. You might say it's an instinctive reflex, but it is not a natural instinct designed as part of your survival toolkit. It's a reflex created by brainwashing. If we do something enough times, the brain is rewired.

So how do we distinguish the natural survival instincts from the unnatural reaction to being brainwashed? It's actually a case of distinguishing fact from fiction.

The brainwashing creates the belief in your mind that smoking offers some kind of pleasure or crutch. The cycle of addiction, whereby each cigarette offers partial relief from the craving created by the one before, convinces you that you do get some pleasure or comfort when you smoke. Remember, this is no more of a pleasure than the relief of taking off tight shoes. But, you might ask, if you believe that you're gaining some pleasure from smoking, what does it matter if that perception is based on fact or fiction?

Would you remain grateful to the thief for giving you $10 of the $100 he secretly stole from you once you found out about his ruse? Of course not.

It matters because smoking does the complete opposite of what you believe.

SMOKING MAKES ALL SMOKERS MISERABLE

BUT YOU ONLY REALIZE JUST HOW MISERABLE WHEN YOU STOP

If the delusion really made you happy, you might argue that it's worth all the money and the risks to your health. But it doesn't. Smoking makes you irritable, self-despising and frightened. And the more you smoke, the worse you feel.

When you satisfy a genuine instinct like hunger or thirst, it gives you genuine pleasure and a lasting feeling of satisfaction and wellbeing. When you smoke, all you get is temporary and partial relief, which is quickly replaced by insecurity and emptiness. This void is created by the very thing that you take to relieve it. But you keep taking it because you believe in the myth. The only way to remove this artificial void is to remove the addiction.

Unravelling the brainwashing so you can distinguish genuine instinctive fact from brainwashed intellectual fiction is actually incredibly easy. All you need to do is channel your intellect in the right direction and use it to replace misinformed responses with correctly informed ones.

Exercise: **SEEING IS BELIEVING**

This is a simple exercise to demonstrate how easy it is to reprogram your brain through the correct application of intellect. Look at the image below, relax your mind and see what you can make of it.

At first glance it looks like a jumble of random black shapes. Now move the book gradually away from your eyes and try to focus on the white space between the shapes. Can you see it yet? If not, half-close your eyes.

You should see the word STOP. Now bring the book closer again and you should still be able to see the word. It's as clear as day, isn't it? So why is it not apparent at first glance?

Your intellect has learned that the relevant text in a book is printed black on white, so you instinctively look for the formation of the black shapes first. All you have to do is reprogram your intellect to look at the white shapes, not the black, and you can quickly see the message.

What's more, once you've seen the STOP message, it's impossible to look at the diagram again and not see it. Your brain knows for a fact that the word is there and you cannot fool your brain into believing that it's not. The same happens when you see through the myth and recognize the truth about smoking – that it does absolutely nothing for you whatsoever. Once you've seen the truth, you can't fool your brain into believing the myth again.

CHANGE YOUR PERCEPTION

To help you see through the myth, it helps to look at your addiction through the eyes of a non-smoker. You can get an idea of how that might appear by thinking about how you regard a heroin addict. Apart from the tiny proportion of smokers who are also addicted to heroin, smokers have no problem in seeing that heroin will do absolutely nothing for them and that they neither need nor want it. You don't have to keep convincing yourself.

So why do you think heroin addicts have this great desire to inject themselves with the drug? Do you envy them? Or do you thank your lucky stars that you're not going through the same hell as them? If you could help them, wouldn't you tell them to stop? Why do you think they can't see their predicament in the same way as you? Could it be because their perspective has been distorted by the drug?

Now consider this: non-smokers regard you and your predicament in exactly the same way. It's clear to them that there is no pleasure and that smoking leaves you feeling more insecure, unrelaxed and distracted. Their perception is not distorted by any drug. They can see the facts as clearly as you just saw the word STOP.

If you're still clinging to the myth that smoking offers you some sort of pleasure or crutch, it's time to change your perception. We're approaching the end of the first day and you should already be seeing your addiction in a new light. It's not enough, though, just to understand the logic in what I've told you so far.

YOU HAVE TO ACCEPT IT

That means questioning everything that you believe to be true about smoking, including what I've told you, and examining it carefully until you see the truth, just as you did with the STOP diagram. This leads us to the second instruction.

SECOND INSTRUCTION:
OPEN YOUR MIND

Perhaps you think you are an open-minded person. But the mind can be easily fooled into believing something that is untrue. Once we believe in something we tend to close our minds to anything that contradicts that belief. The nicotine trap relies on this aspect of human intellect. Only when you question your belief with an open mind can you determine fact from fiction.

Exercise: **A CLASSIC ILLUSION**

Illusions can be fun, as long as they're not responsible for keeping you in a trap. Take a look at these two tables. Make a note of which is the longer, A or B?

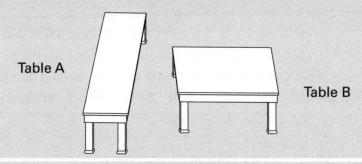

Table A

Table B

Now take a ruler and measure the tables. Surprising, isn't it?

What you're looking at is a famous optical illusion, whereby the tables are drawn in such a way as to look very different in dimension when, in fact, they are identical. Had you not been told to measure them you would have carried on with the assumption that they are different sizes.

Now try this. Look at the tables again and try to convince yourself that they really are different sizes.

Impossible, isn't it?

In the last session of the day we will strip away any lingering doubts so you end the day not only understanding but fully believing that the myth is false and the truth is clear:

SMOKING DOES NOTHING FOR YOU WHATSOEVER

FIRST STEPS TO FREEDOM

YOU MAY BE WONDERING HOW YOU CAN UNDO A LIFETIME'S BRAINWASHING IN JUST FOUR DAYS. DON'T WORRY, WE NORMALLY SUCCEED IN AROUND FIVE HOURS AT OUR LIVE SEMINARS. LIKE ANYTHING THAT IS NOT BUILT ON SOLID FOUNDATIONS, THE BRAINWASHING IS AS FRAGILE AS A HOUSE OF CARDS AND WILL COLLAPSE IN AN INSTANT. ALL YOU HAVE TO DO IS GIVE IT A SHAKE.

NO MORE STOPPING AND STARTING

Changing your mindset is all it takes to remove the desire to smoke. We now have a simple set of tasks.

1. Identify what's wrong with your current mindset

2. Remove that from your way of thinking

3. Let logic and reason undo the brainwashing

Logic and reasoning are your dynamite. When you apply them to your reasons for smoking, the whole argument collapses and you are left with no lingering desire to smoke. The problem for smokers is that they don't apply logic and reason because the addiction distorts their sense of reality.

This method shows you how to apply logic and reason. It's as simple as that. Easyway shows you how to light the fuse to bring the brainwashing collapsing down.

Our objective is to help you quit PERMANENTLY. How many times have you vowed that you're going to quit smoking, only to fall into the trap again?

Smokers are notorious for repeatedly stopping and starting. To the non-smoker, this is illogical. If you like smoking, why keep trying to quit? If you don't like smoking, why keep starting again?

Falling back into the trap is not like falling into a physical trap. If you fell into a pit of stagnant water, you would make sure you didn't go anywhere near that pit again, wouldn't you? But the nicotine trap is not a physical trap; it's a mental trap, based on illusion.

Smokers who stop and start again have not seen through the illusion.

All smokers wish they could quit. That's why they're always trying to do so. As well as all the logical reasons for quitting – the health risks, the cost, the smell, etc. – you know it doesn't make you happy. On the contrary, it makes you feel like a miserable slave.

Yet despite this, the smokers who stop and start again never remove the desire for cigarettes. They haven't seen through the myth. Like someone who looks at the black shapes and can't see the word STOP, they're still being fooled by the illusion. It's as illogical as thinking there's a good reason for falling into a pit of stagnant water, but addiction overrides logic.

Do you want to be a non-smoker? Then you need to understand the one real difference between smokers and non-smokers. It's not that non-smokers have been spared the brainwashing – they haven't. Neither is it that they had the willpower to resist getting hooked – you don't need willpower to be a non-smoker. Nor that they are wired differently – it has nothing to do with genetics. The real difference is that non-smokers never have the desire to smoke.

Anyone who retains a desire to smoke will feel deprived if they can't smoke. They will need willpower to fight the feeling of deprivation and they will be forever vulnerable to falling back into the trap when their willpower runs out.

Remove your desire to smoke and you will become a happy non-smoker

EASILY, IMMEDIATELY AND PAINLESSLY

You won't need willpower.

People who have never been smokers don't have the desire to smoke, though they may still be tempted to try. They have been subjected to all the brainwashing and they may believe that there must be some pleasure or crutch in smoking, but they have been able to make a logical choice not to subject themselves to the world's number one killer because their mind is not controlled by nicotine addiction.

People who become happy non-smokers with Easyway also have no desire to smoke. They have an advantage over people who have never smoked because they *know* there is no pleasure or crutch to be gained from smoking and they have not had to use reason to outweigh temptation.

EASYWAY REMOVES THE TEMPTATION TO SMOKE ALTOGETHER

When you know for a fact that smoking does absolutely nothing for you whatsoever, any desire disappears. See through the myth and it becomes easy to avoid falling into the trap again. Once you're free, you'll be more likely to start believing in Santa Claus again than fall back into the trap. All you need to do is follow the instructions.

HARD DRUGS

Despite the fact that cigarettes are responsible for far more deaths than heroin, we regard heroin as a hard drug and nicotine as a social drug. I'm not suggesting you start taking heroin and even if I did, I doubt you would pay any attention. More likely you would throw the book away and write me off as a madman.

We're talking about a drug that is very dangerous. People make a fortune from selling it and deliberately try to get their customers hooked so they have a steadily increasing income. It's highly addictive and if you try it you're likely to get hooked straight away, and remain hooked for the rest of your life.

It's also very expensive: the average addict spends over $140,000 (£100,000) in their lifetime. But whatever the cost, they always make sure they find the money, regardless of what other sacrifices they have to make.

When you take the drug, you become increasingly lethargic, short of breath and your immune system weakens, leaving you susceptible to all sorts of diseases. Worst of all, it destroys your nervous system by stealth, as well as your courage, your confidence and your ability to concentrate. It makes you despise yourself for being a slave to something you detest, but the more it drags you down, the more you depend on it.

And what does this drug do for you? Absolutely nothing. Not one single thing.

A couple more points: it tastes awful, causes bad breath, stained teeth, wheezing, coughing, shame and guilt; and it wipes out 7 million people per year worldwide.

That's right, I'm not talking about heroin; I'm talking about nicotine. If I tried to sell you a drug using the description above, would you buy it? Or would you throw me out, just like you would if I tried to persuade you to take heroin? After all, who in their right mind would cough up such a fortune to put themselves through all that misery?

We have no difficulty in seeing heroin addiction as a vile, pitiful, deadly condition, yet we have a distorted view of smoking or vaping. We need to make sure you can see your addiction exactly as you see the heroin addict's addiction. To do this, you need to disregard the images portrayed in society. It's easy to associate heroin with addiction, slavery, poverty, misery, squalor and death because you haven't been bombarded with images of happy, laughing heroin addicts. Smokers, on the other hand, are portrayed as cool, in control, stylish, beautiful people. The inference is that these smokers are happy because they're smoking.

It's essential that you see through this illusion. You don't just need to tell yourself it's untrue; you *know* it's untrue because you know how smoking makes you feel. Disregard the popular image of smokers and look at your own evidence. Look at the smokers you know in real life. How many of them look and behave like movie stars?

And remember, the people on screen are actually fictional. Off screen those actors who really smoke are just as miserable as you are. And the ones who don't will be reaching for the mouthwash as soon as they get off set.

FEAR OF SUCCESS

From tomorrow, we will begin the process of stripping away the illusions that have kept you in the nicotine trap. Our goal is the removal of all your doubts about wanting to quit. Those doubts are fuelled by the chief ally of addiction:

FEAR

Smokers are held back from trying to quit by numerous fears:

• Fear of being unable to enjoy meals, drinks or social occasions

• Fear of being unable to handle stress

• Fear of being unable to concentrate

• Fear of having to go through some terrible trauma to get free

• Fear of having to resist temptation for the rest of their life

They fear that they won't have the resilience to cope with these challenges and so any attempt to quit will end in dismal failure. What they're really afraid of is success.

The fear of failure is a spur. It drives actors to learn their lines, athletes to practise their skills, pilots to check their instruments, etc., etc. There is no logic in not trying to quit because you're afraid of failure. The calamity you're afraid of has already happened.

YOU ARE A SMOKER!

By not trying to quit, you guarantee that the unthinkable happens. You remain a smoker. Instead, think about everything you stand to gain. How proud will your family and friends be? More importantly, how proud will you feel?

The fears listed above amount to the fear of success. "If I quit, life will be tough." Smokers have been fooled into thinking cigarettes provide them with a crutch in stressful situations and that there will be no pleasure in life without them. The thought of never having another cigarette is frightening.

Non-smokers manage to enjoy life and cope with stressful situations. In fact, they cope better and enjoy life more. The only reason you might think life will be worse without cigarettes is because your addiction makes you miserable when you don't smoke. As long as you continue to feed the Little Monster, this will be the case. Lose the cigarettes and the fear goes too.

You are one day into your four-day Easyway Boot Camp and you may be finding it hard to imagine just how good life will be without smoking. Believe me, you will soon be looking back on this moment thinking, "I can't believe I feel this good."

Not only will you feel more healthy and energetic but you will also notice a marked improvement in your confidence, courage and concentration too.

A POSITIVE APPROACH

So far, we have concentrated on preparing your mindset to unravel the brainwashing and strip away the illusions that have kept you trapped. Before we finish for the day, there are two further instructions as you look forward to making your escape.

THIRD INSTRUCTION: THINK POSITIVE

If you have been wrestling with the fear of success, there will be concerns in your mind about what you are about to achieve. Smokers who think they are going to be required to make a sacrifice will approach the attempt to quit with a sense of doom and gloom. There is no reason to feel miserable.

YOU ARE NOT GIVING UP ANYTHING

Instead you are making wonderful gains. Every smoker dreams of waking up in the morning with the sense of freedom you will feel when you complete this course. As you go to bed tonight, allow yourself to imagine how good life is going to be and get excited about what you are about to achieve. This is a fantastic moment in your life.

FOURTH INSTRUCTION: BEGIN, NOT WITH A FEELING OF DOOM AND GLOOM, BUT INSTEAD WITH A FEELING OF ELATION AND EXCITEMENT

Remember, if you follow all the instructions, nothing can stop you from escaping. Let go of the fear and get free.

CHECKLIST

I understand that:

○ The only reason I smoke is to feed the Little Monster – addiction.

○ I am in an ingenious trap that makes me think smoking gives me pleasure and/or a crutch when, in fact, it does the opposite.

○ The physical nicotine cravings of the Little Monster are so minute as to be almost imperceptible. I've lived with them throughout my smoking life.

○ It's the Big Monster that interprets those cravings as "I want a cigarette".

○ Escape will be easy if I follow all the instructions.

○ All I have to do is kill the Big Monster. The Little Monster will quickly die once I starve it of nicotine.

○ The fear of failure is illogical.

○ The fear of success is caused by nicotine addiction and brainwashing. Remove them and the fear goes too.

UNRAVELLING THE BRAINWASHING

Yesterday we established the real reasons you smoke. You are now armed with the knowledge that when you started smoking you were dragged into a trap: nicotine addiction. This trap distorts logic and tricks its victims into believing that relief from their restlessness lies in the very thing that's causing it: smoking. You should now understand that the really unpleasant and noticeable physical feelings you've felt in the past when you attempted to quit were not caused by nicotine withdrawal, but were the physical reaction to a mental process which is in itself triggered by the extremely mild physical withdrawal of nicotine.

The Little Monster (the physical withdrawal) is a virtually imperceptible feeling, so slight most smokers aren't even aware of it while they sleep. This very slight physical feeling (the Little Monster) pokes the Big Monster (the brainwashing and the mental process), which creates unpleasant physical feelings.

It works like this:

Physical withdrawal

↓

Mental process:
"I want a cigarette but can't have one."

↓

Physical unpleasantness: "AGGGH"

Today's task is to begin the process of releasing you from the nicotine trap by dismantling the myth that smoking provides some sort of pleasure or crutch. It is this myth that creates the desire to smoke. Remove that desire and escape from the trap is easy.

The myth is reinforced by a number of other myths that are put out there as facts by tobacco companies and anti-smoking campaigners alike. With your mind corrupted by these myths, it's no wonder you have been unable to quit smoking up until now.

Today we are going to tackle seven of these myths:

• **That smoking or vaping helps you relax**

• **That you can't quit without willpower**

• **That quitting requires you to make a sacrifice**

• **That you might have an addictive personality**

• **That smoking or vaping helps you concentrate**

- That smoking or vaping helps with weight control and appetite suppression

- That smoking or vaping reduces depression or is an expression of self-harm

By the time we've finished dismantling these myths, you will be feeling much more confident about your ability to quit easily, painlessly and permanently. That's a very exciting feeling. You can begin to imagine life without cigarettes or any form of nicotine; you'll be healthier, more energetic, better off, free.

So let's get started. Remember to follow all the instructions. Keep an open mind, make no assumptions and question everything. The truth will become obvious. And remember to carry on smoking or vaping while you read. I don't want you to waste any time or brainpower wondering whether you should or shouldn't do so. Just carry on as you are until you're ready to smoke your final cigarette or e-cigarette. I'll guide you through that amazing ritual when the time comes. And please don't worry if the prospect makes you nervous or anxious – that's perfectly understandable. This Boot Camp programme is exactly the length it needs to be... if we could achieve the result in fewer words, we'd do so. So stick with it, regardless of how positive or negative you feel; you have absolutely nothing to lose and everything to gain.

DAY TWO: CHAPTER ONE
THE ILLUSION OF PLEASURE

AS LONG AS YOU STICK WITH THE BELIEF THAT SMOKING GIVES YOU SOME SORT OF PLEASURE OR CRUTCH, YOU WILL NOT BE ABLE TO FREE YOURSELF FROM THE NICOTINE TRAP. IT'S ESSENTIAL, THEN, FOR ME TO BEGIN THE DAY BY MAKING SURE YOU FULLY UNDERSTAND THAT ANY PLEASURE YOU THINK YOU GET FROM SMOKING IS AN ILLUSION.

I'm going to make a powerful statement:
YOU HAVEN'T ENJOYED A SINGLE CIGARETTE OR E-CIGARETTE YOU'VE EVER SMOKED!

Now don't get me wrong – there's no doubt that you've "enjoyed" tremendous "relief" when lighting a cigarette after a long period of time without one; after a long flight, train journey, or an attempt to quit. Yet that feeling of enjoyment and relief is nothing more than the feeling you'd get if you wore shoes that were a size too small all day. It would feel fabulous when you took them off. But would you do that? Of course not! We go out of our way to select our shoes carefully – so they fit just right.

You owe nicotine absolutely nothing. No more than you'd be grateful to the thief who stole $100 from you and "gifted" you $10… once you discovered the con, you'd never be grateful to the thief again.

PLEASURE OR CRUTCH?

It is widely assumed, by smokers and non-smokers alike, that the effect of smoking must deliver something positive – otherwise why would people keep doing it?

We all know the dangers of smoking: nobody is trying to deny that it is the world's number one killer, a major cause of cancer, heart disease and emphysema, in addition to the asthma, coughing, wheezing, lack of stamina and numerous other ailments that smokers and vapers put up with in order to keep getting their fix – so the assumption is that there must be something pretty special about it to make smokers disregard all these negatives and carry on spending vast amounts of money on cigarettes.

The perceived pleasure of smoking lies in the way a cigarette seems to enhance social occasions, make drinks more enjoyable, round off a meal or just put the finishing touch to a relaxing, satisfying moment. The perceived crutch lies in the cigarette's ability to help you relax, take your mind off the stresses of life and concentrate.

In fact, all these perceived pleasures and crutches are illusory. Cigarettes, e-cigarettes, dip, and in fact any nicotine product actually do nothing of the sort.

On the contrary, they are antisocial; they ruin the taste of meals and drinks; they make a relaxing situation feel edgy; they add to your stress and they destroy your concentration. You only have to observe how embarrassed most vapers are when using their devices. It only becomes less embarrassing when they are in the company of other addicts. That's why smokers and vapers seem to have that camaraderie at parties. It's a case of "Thank goodness – I'm not the only one here!"

But let's examine the claim that smoking or vaping can help you to take your mind off things at times of stress and help you concentrate at a time when you're required to focus. Think about it: how can the same drug take your mind off things and help you concentrate at the same time?

The same person who claims that smoking distracts their mind in a stressful situation will, in the next breath, also claim that it provides no distraction whatsoever when it comes to concentration – in fact they claim it helps them to do so. If you haven't immediately grasped the contradictory nature of those two claims, then please read the last two paragraphs again before moving on.

There is no genuine pleasure or crutch to be derived from smoking or vaping; we only think there is because of the brainwashing and the way the nicotine trap twists our perception.

The fact is, our addiction to nicotine makes us incapable of doing anything without a cigarette before, during, or after a stressful or focus-requiring event. It's like that neighbour's burglar alarm that goes off for hours, and the feeling of relief when it finally stops. That is the only reason you believe that nicotine helps you to focus (you are removing the aggravation of wanting a cigarette) and the only reason you believe it helps you cope with stress (you constantly have the aggravation of wanting a cigarette and if you can't have a cigarette it actually adds to your stress levels).

Am I really expecting you to believe that nobody ever enjoyed a single cigarette? It seems too far-fetched. How could anyone create an illusion on such a massive scale?

It's all to do with every smoker's reluctance to admit to their misery. Instead of admitting to being a helpless slave, they choose to perpetuate the myth that smoking gives them some kind of pleasure or crutch. There is no need for putting a brave face on it in this Boot Camp. You're in it together with all the other smokers on the planet, but you can admit the truth here: smoking does nothing for you whatsoever.

Although I expect you're beginning to understand exactly what I mean, please don't worry if you require further evidence. Every doubt, every question on your mind at this point will be covered before I ask you to smoke your final cigarette, e-cigarette, or take nicotine in whatever form it is that you're addicted to. So let's examine those illusions and make sure we can see through them.

I ENJOY THE SMELL AND TASTE

Some people say they like the smell of cigarette smoke. Is that reason enough to poison yourself and risk getting cancer, heart disease, emphysema and all the other horrible diseases that smoking can cause? I like the smell of roses, but I could easily live without it. If my life depended on never smelling another rose again, I would have absolutely no problem going along with that. I'm sure you feel the same.

When a smoker quits with the willpower method and is desperately trying to resist the temptation to smoke, the smell of a cigarette might be enough to make them crack but that's not because they adore the smell of cigarettes more than life itself. It's because they associate the smell with the relief of the craving for nicotine.

Most smokers can't stand the smell of other people's smoke. They only tolerate the smell of their own because it's a signal that they're getting their fix.

Don't become obsessed with the idea that you like the smell of smoke. It probably sounds weird, but I like the smell of gasoline but I don't hang around gas stations or carry a small bottle of petroleum on me to sniff it every now and then. It doesn't matter if you like the smell;

all that matters is that you get rid of the belief that you smoke because you like the smell. That's not why you smoke. You smoke in spite of the smell rather than because of it.

Vaping is no different. Although you might believe that you love the smell of your butterscotch, bubblegum, cotton candy, or gummy bear "vape juice", I can assure you that no one is following you around attempting to inhale it themselves. The smell in this case isn't from a relatively benign source such as a candy store (who doesn't love the smell that blows out of those?); in the case of a vape cloud its source is revolting.

One of the therapists at our London centre came up with an excellent analogy. He asserted that it's more likely that someone would eat a "camel dung sandwich" if it smelt like bananas or strawberries and cream. But essentially it doesn't change the fact that it's a camel dung sandwich and as soon as someone is made aware of that, no one, not even someone on one of those weird TV programmes where participants are set repulsive eating challenges, would actually eat it.

Nicotine is a poison. When you smoke, you take toxic fumes into your mouth, nose and lungs. The first time you ever inhale smoke it makes you choke and gag, at least a little; the poison is that foul. It's not a taste that makes you think, "I could get hooked on this if I'm not careful." On the contrary, it's so foul that you feel confident you could never get hooked on it.

You smoke the second and third cigarettes because you want to be able to smoke without choking and gagging. You've been brainwashed into thinking it's cool, stylish, grown-up… so you persevere. Eventually the cigarettes no longer make you choke. You call it "acquiring the taste". All you've done is acquire a lack of taste. Your immune system has built a tolerance to the poison, so you're less sensitive to the foul taste and smell. By this stage, you're well and truly hooked and smoking not because you want to be a smoker but because you're being controlled by addiction.

Most cigarettes are smoked without the smoker paying any attention at all to the taste or smell. In fact, most smokers struggle to taste anything. When you become a non-smoker you will rediscover just how good food tastes. After years of knocking out your taste buds, your natural survival toolkit will quickly recover its full capacity.

As a smoker, the taste and smell of everything is dulled because of the way your body's natural defences protect you from poison by building a tolerance. If you notice that a meal you're eating in a restaurant is too salty, check outside the kitchen door later and you'll be sure to find a chef who smokes. It destroys the palate – it doesn't enhance it. No one smokes because they enjoy the taste or smell; they only think they do because they associate the taste and smell with the illusion of relief and the illusion of pleasure that they suffer as a nicotine addict.

MY SPECIAL CIGARETTES

One of the strongest illusions smokers suffer is that there are certain relaxed occasions when a cigarette tastes particularly special. Typical occasions are first thing in the morning, after a meal, with a drink, during a break at work, when you first get home, after exercise and after sex.

These are all classic occasions when smokers rush to light up with relish, eager to mark the moment by sucking poisonous fumes into their lungs. All these occasions have one thing in common: they follow a period of abstinence. The Little Monster has been kept waiting longer than usual, so it is constantly prodding the Big Monster, and so the feeling of relief seems greater as a consequence.

The first cigarette in the morning is a strange one. It actually tastes revolting and makes you wheeze, cough and feel lousier than any other cigarette of the day. It seems special because you've gone without nicotine for hours. So strong is the human body that it has started to recover overnight, so it is more sensitive to the poison. Smokers talk about the hit they get from that first smoke of the day. This is actually their body recoiling from the poison.

Other smokers talk about the "buzz" or "high" from a cigarette in these situations. Wake up! That isn't a buzz or a high – it's just a dizzy sensation caused by lack of oxygen to your brain and the poisoning effect of the nicotine. You can get exactly the same feeling by holding your breath for longer than is comfortable or from spinning around in a circle for 20 seconds. Calling it a buzz or a high is just something we do in a vain attempt to justify our smoking. If you've ever experienced one of life's *REAL* highs, you'll know that the notion of a high caused by nicotine is a nonsense.

Going back to those special occasions, ask yourself this: would those moments cease to be special if you took away the cigarette?

How does a non-smoker feel after a meal? They feel GREAT! How does a smoker or vaper feel if they're unable to smoke or vape at that time? LOUSY. They light a cigarette and how do they feel? GREAT! In other words – they feel the same as a non-smoker feels! Get it?

How does a non-smoker feel when they hook up with some friends in a bar or coffee shop? GREAT! How does a smoker or vaper feel in that same situation if they're unable to smoke or vape? LOUSY! How do they feel when they're able to take their fix of nicotine? GREAT! Like a non-smoker feels all the time.

I'll keep going for a little longer. By now I hope you understand exactly what I'm saying, but let's make sure.

How does a non-smoker feel after sex? FABULOUS! How does a smoker feel if they're unable to smoke? LOUSY! They have a cigarette and feel fabulous... like a non-smoker feels. Actually, this example differs slightly in that often a smoker will "get love-making over with" as a matter of urgency – just as soon as the thought of a cigarette enters their mind... Meanwhile, while the smoker's lighting up their post-coital cigarette, the happy non-smoker is happily carrying on, or enjoying doing it all over again, or simply lying wrapped in their lover's arms. You can see why sometimes having a partner who smokes can be very frustrating and unrewarding for a non-smoker.

Incidentally, if your partner smokes and has no intention of quitting, or fails to quit at the same time as you, please don't worry. Other than the issue mentioned above, which I'm sure love will conquer, it won't cause you a problem.

In the past if they've carried on smoking when you attempted to quit, it might have made you envious or caused temptation because cigarettes were always around the house, but this time you're going to be truly free, not remotely tempted to smoke, so it really won't bother you if your partner, friends or colleagues continue.

More about special cigarettes, like the one during a break from work: well... there's no doubt that there is great camaraderie among smokers in the smoking shelter at work. So after you've quit, make sure you carry on taking those breaks. Go for a "no-smoke-break". You don't want to miss out on the chat and the gossip and the friendship of those breaks just because you've quit smoking. The great thing about being a happy non-smoker is that you can choose when to take your breaks, rather than be compelled to by the Little Monster and the Big Monster. If it's pouring down with rain or freezing cold, you can give it a miss. You can pick and choose when and where to take a break. Other than the phoney relief of the addiction, it's the break that the smoker enjoys – not the cigarette.

When you stop smoking you will discover that all these scenarios are not only special regardless of the cigarette; they are actually more special without it.

As a smoker or vaper, you're never fully relaxed. Therefore, smoking actually spoils relaxing situations by adding an unnecessary layer of stress. Which brings us to the next popular myth.

SMOKING OR VAPING EASES MY STRESS

How can something that creates stress ease stress?

Whenever you smoke you feed the Little Monster and thus give yourself some temporary relief from the craving. When you don't understand the nature of the trap you're in, you interpret this relief as a genuine easing of your stress level. Before the cigarette you feel stressed; as you smoke the cigarette you feel less stressed. And so you jump to the simple and obvious conclusion.

But think back to the table illusion from yesterday. The obvious is not always the truth, particularly if you've only been given one way of looking at it.

Stress is a fact of life, suffered by smokers and non-smokers alike. But smokers suffer an additional layer of stress caused by nicotine withdrawal (the Little Monster) which triggers the even worse feeling of stress (the Big Monster: "I want a cigarette – I can't have one – AGGH!"). When you light up, you partially relieve this additional layer of stress. But smoking makes no impact on genuine stress. The truth is it adds to it.

I can guarantee that…

YOU WILL BE LESS STRESSED AS A NON-SMOKER

The additional layer of stress is responsible for every smoker's descent into the nicotine trap. Like the fly in the pitcher plant, once you're in the nicotine trap there is only one way to go: down.

UNLESS, OF COURSE, YOU CHOOSE TO ESCAPE

The natural tendency with any addictive drug is to take more, not less. This is because of your body's incredible ability to build a tolerance to the poison. Because of this tolerance, each cigarette can give only partial relief from the nicotine craving. You become increasingly desensitized to the poison, so it takes more of the drug to get the same effect. You inhale deeper and more frequently, reduce the gap between cigarettes and switch to stronger brands.

WELLBEING

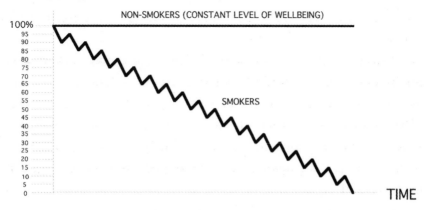

The graph on the previous page illustrates the smoker's descent as time goes by. Let's say that your level of stress was "normal" before you started smoking. This is indicated as 100 per cent on the diagram. As you experience withdrawal from that first cigarette, you feel a low. You dip down below 100 per cent. Your next cigarette relieves this feeling but not completely because of your tolerance to the poison. You certainly couldn't call it a high. At best it's partial and temporary relief. So you don't quite make it back to 100 per cent. The next withdrawal causes a low that takes you down further than before. So the pattern continues, taking you down further and further with each cigarette.

All the while, those periods of partial relief are fooling you into thinking you're getting some pleasure from the cigarettes. You keep believing the myth. But with each cigarette you're falling further and further below "normal", each time setting yourself a new normal lower than the one before. Meanwhile, your stress level is increasing and your health is deteriorating. You start to feel lethargic and out of breath. You develop a cough and a wheeze. You start to see cancer as a probability rather than an unthinkable risk. This adds another layer of stress, so now you're experiencing a double low.

As your descent accelerates, you have to admit to yourself that you're a slave; you're not smoking because you choose to; the cigarettes are controlling your life. This feeling of helplessness adds to your misery. Now it's a triple low. Like the fly, you're gazing into the pit and resigning yourself to a miserable end.

But the great news is that, unlike the fly, you *can* escape. And you can do so any time you choose. You're not in a physical trap – the nicotine trap is entirely of your own making and it exists in your mind. In fact you are your own jailer. Change your mindset and you can walk free easily, immediately and painlessly

Even better, when you escape the trap, your health and mental wellbeing will bounce back up very quickly. All that added stress will lift from your shoulders, you will enjoy the feeling of renewed health and vigour, not to mention more money, and you will experience a feeling of elation.

YIPPEE! I'M FREE!

When you're smoking, you have to suppress your instincts and bury your head in the sand. That's the only way you can maintain the illusion of pleasure. You have to block out the foul taste and smell, the money you're wasting, the slavery and the knowledge that the next cigarette could be the one that triggers cancer. The pretence is very stressful. When you quit, you don't have to go through that any more. The relief is incredible.

Exercise: **LET GO OF UNNECESSARY STRESS**

It's the additional layers of stress that make smokers miserable. The fear of what smoking is doing to you and the misery of being a slave are stresses that non-smokers and non-vapers don't suffer. You don't have to suffer them either, now that you know you're on the way to becoming a happy non-smoker. Just the aggravation of working out when and where you can have your next cigarette or e-cigarette adds significantly to your stress levels. I used to break journeys unnecessarily just so I could have a cigarette. I'd juggle my whole day around when and where I could smoke. For a chain-smoker, it's like having an extra full-time job.

Next time you think about the effect your smoking or vaping is having on you, let the thought pass without allowing it to make you feel anxious. There is no need to worry any more because you are escaping from the trap. Replace your anxiety with a feeling of anticipation or elation. Instead of letting your thoughts about smoking become a source of stress, think about all the marvellous gains you're about to make and use the thought as a source of joy.

"I'M NOT GOING TO BE A SLAVE ANY MORE. I'M GOING TO BE FREE!"

I ENJOY THE RITUAL

A lot of people are attracted to smoking by the paraphernalia. Cigarette packets, lighters, boxes of matches, ashtrays, etc. Vaping has created the same kind of thing based around which device, which "vape juice", which flavour? All have a certain style that appeals to young people in need of an identity. A lot of long-term smokers will also tell you that this is what they enjoy about smoking. The inference is that they wouldn't smoke if it wasn't for the ritual of opening the packet, handling the cigarette, striking the lighter…

I want you to go through your usual ritual now. Focus on each part of it: opening the packet, taking out a cigarette, putting it between your lips. Do everything you usually do. Take your lighter. Light the cigarette. Are you paying attention?

OK, now stop. Stub out the cigarette immediately, without taking another puff. Put the lighter away. How do you feel? If you're worried about wasting a cigarette by only having one puff, don't even light it. Just put it straight back in the packet. Are you satisfied?

I suspect you're not. No smoker smokes for the ritual. If they did they would be happy to stop short of lighting the cigarette. Imagine that! You could spare yourself all the harmful part and still have the enjoyment.

But it doesn't work like that, does it? Smokers only enjoy the ritual of smoking because it's a necessary route to getting their fix. Remember, the only reason anyone smokes or vapes or uses dip or any other nicotine device is to get the nicotine.

IT'S JUST A HABIT

When smokers find themselves running out of excuses, they resort to a more resigned explanation as to why they smoke. "It's just a habit." They're no longer trying to convince themselves or anyone else that they're in control, but there is still the implication that smoking gives them some kind of pleasure or crutch. It's essential to understand that you smoke because you're addicted to a drug and drug addiction is not a habit.

A habit is a repeated behaviour that you do for the familiarity and comfort of repetition. But you don't smoke for the comfort of repetition; you smoke to get nicotine to relieve the withdrawal pangs from the previous cigarette and ease the mental aggravation caused by the Big Monster.

If you believe that you smoke because you've fallen into the habit, you will find it hard to quit. You will assume that it's just a weakness in your nature that has made you susceptible to the habit. But when you accept that smoking is an addiction and you understand the nature of the nicotine trap, it's easy to follow the instructions to escape.

Get this clear in your mind, the habit of smoking might trigger the thought of having a cigarette, but that's not why you smoke. In the past, when you've attempted to quit, the habit trigger has caused you to mope for a cigarette, but remember that was when your Big Monster was still alive; you missed cigarettes; you felt deprived. This time when you quit, you won't feel like you're missing out on anything, so if you habitually experience a trigger, getting off a bus for example, it'll be a moment of happiness, a moment you can remind yourself how lucky you are to be free, rather than a moment for concern. I know you'll find that hard to believe at this point, but I'm sure you understand exactly what I'm saying, just on principle. That's all you need to do as we work through this programme.

A further problem with seeing smoking as a habit is that it encourages the belief that you can moderate it, so you can have the occasional cigarette without falling into the trap again. Get it clear in your mind:

THERE IS NO SUCH THING AS "JUST THE ONE"

If you smoke one, what's to stop you smoking the next one, and the next? If you retain the desire for just one cigarette, you will not escape the trap.

EASYWAY REMOVES TEMPTATION

The belief that you smoke out of habit makes smokers feel stupid. One part of your brain is telling you, "You're a fool. Stop doing it!" Another part is saying, "I'm helpless to resist the temptation."

In fact, smokers are not stupid. They are being conned by a fiendish force called addiction. The temptation exists because you have been brainwashed into believing a myth: that smoking gives you some kind of pleasure or crutch. Even when you reach the point where you can no longer convince yourself that you are getting any pleasure or crutch from smoking, the temptation to go on smoking remains. It is driven by fear. "How will I be able to cope without cigarettes?"

What smokers don't realize is that the cigarette, far from relieving this fear, causes it. Non-smokers don't suffer it. The problem is that it works back to front. It's when you're not smoking that you notice the empty, insecure feeling that smoking causes. When you light up, the feeling is partially relieved and your brain is fooled into believing that the cigarette is your friend. This is how smoking creates the illusion of pleasure.

The more it drags you down, the more you believe you need your "friend" and the more dependent on the drug you become.

In order to remove the temptation, all you have to do is see through the illusion of pleasure. Recognize that the empty, insecure feeling you experience when you're not smoking is nicotine craving caused by smoking and that the "pleasure" you feel when you smoke is merely the temporary and partial relief of that craving and the pacification of the Big Monster in your mind.

Exercise: **DEFINE THE PLEASURE**

Assuming you've continued to smoke as you've been reading the book, light a cigarette now and inhale six deep, glorious lungfuls of the carcinogenic filth. Ask yourself what is so pleasant. What are you actually enjoying about it?

If you vape, do the same. What are you actually enjoying about it?

Remember, this is the little pleasure or crutch that you thought you couldn't live without. Now is your chance to really identify what that pleasure or crutch amounts to. Hold the smoke or vape in your mouth or lungs and focus on the taste. Let the smoke or vape linger in your nostrils or mouth and focus on the smell. Is it pleasant?

You may well feel a sense of relaxation. It's the same as taking off tight shoes. Would you deliberately wear tight shoes, just for the relief of taking them off?

BELIEF NOT WILLPOWER

MOST PEOPLE BELIEVE THAT SMOKERS WHO FAIL TO QUIT LACK THE WILLPOWER TO MAKE THE NECESSARY SACRIFICE. WHEN YOU QUIT WITH EASYWAY, THERE IS NO SACRIFICE AND SO YOU DON'T NEED WILLPOWER. IN FACT, THE WILLPOWER METHOD IS MORE LIKELY TO MAKE YOUR ADDICTION WORSE.

THE WRONG METHOD

So the solution to ending the nicotine craving is NOT to smoke or vape. That way you break the cycle of addiction, kill the Little Monster and get free. Wait a minute! Isn't that what all smokers do when they try to quit? Why doesn't it work for them? If it's so easy to quit, why do so many people find it incredibly hard?

SIMPLE: THEY'RE USING THE WRONG METHOD.

It's not their fault. A fundamental part of the brainwashing is the myth that it's hard to quit. Just about every so-called expert says so, thus adding to every smoker's fear of trying to quit. "I'm going to have to go through some terrible trauma."

This brainwashing is so powerful that smokers actually feel suspicious when they're told that Easyway can help them quit easily and without willpower. It goes against everything they've ever been told about smoking and it sounds too good to be true. Believe me, that is not the case and I will explain why. With Easyway, there is no painful withdrawal period, no traumatic wrestling match with the continuing desire to smoke. With Easyway, you remove the desire completely.

The simplest of tasks becomes difficult if you go about it the wrong way. Opening a door, for example. You know how to open a door – you push on the handle and it swings open with the minimum of effort. But have you ever come across a door with no handle and pushed on the wrong side, where the hinges are? You're met with firm resistance. The door might budge a tiny bit, but it won't swing open. It requires a huge amount of effort and determination. Push on the correct side and the door opens without you even having to think about it.

Most smokers find it difficult to stop because they use the willpower method. They choose the difficult method because they've been brainwashed into believing that is the only way to quit. The method assumes that while the nicotine is leaving your body, you need to be strong-willed to get through two ordeals:

1. The painful withdrawal period

2. The sacrifice of your pleasure or crutch

You should now be able to see the flaws in this theory. Firstly, there is no physical pain with nicotine withdrawal. Smokers go through it every moment that they're not smoking every day of their smoking lives. You barely notice it.

The second flaw in the willpower theory is the assumption that quitting involves a sacrifice. This is only true if you regard the cigarette as your friend. But when you can see through the illusion that smoking gives you pleasure or a crutch and you know that smoking does absolutely nothing for you whatsoever, there is no sense of sacrifice.

Whenever the thought of smoking enters your mind, you don't mope because you can't smoke; you rejoice because you no longer have to. You're not "giving up" anything on Day Four – you're getting rid of something that's plagued your life.

TIGHTENING THE ROPE

People who try to quit with the willpower method constantly endure the tug-of-war of fear. You kill the Little Monster but leave the Big Monster alive. On one side, your rational brain knows you should stop smoking because it's making you ill, costing you a fortune, controlling your life and making you miserable. On the other side your addicted brain makes you panic at the thought of being deprived of your pleasure or crutch. On the willpower method you focus on all the reasons for stopping and hope you can last long enough without smoking for the desire to eventually go.

Some people do manage to stop smoking through sheer force of will, but they don't become happy non-smokers. They never actually break free of their addiction, and so they are always fighting the temptation to fall back into the pit.

In most cases, the willpower method fails and you end up feeling more helpless and miserable than before.

With the willpower method, the struggle never ends. It becomes an ordeal, like running a marathon – except there is no finish line. You're forever waiting for something NOT to happen so you never feel the elation of knowing you're free. With Easyway, you know you're a happy non-smoker the moment you kill the Big Monster and smoke your final cigarette.

As long as you continue to believe that you're giving something up, you will always be running in pain. The stronger your will, the longer you will withstand the agony.

The longer you go on suffering a sense of deprivation, the more powerful your craving for a cigarette becomes.

The feeling of deprivation makes you miserable, which in turn increases your desire for a cigarette – the crutch you always used to turn to in a crisis. You only have to succumb to this temptation once and all that hard work is wasted. Worse still, once you've failed on the willpower method, it's even harder to try again.

Failing to quit with the willpower method leaves you more addicted than before because it reinforces the belief that it is impossible to cure your problem. People will tell you they felt an enormous sense of relief when they gave in and had that first cigarette, but this relief is nothing more than a temporary end to the self-inflicted pain.

Nobody thinks, "Great! I'm smoking again!" It is not a pleasure. In fact, it is accompanied by strong feelings of failure and foreboding, guilt and disappointment. Any hope you had that you might be free of the tyranny of smoking is snuffed out in that moment.

If you believe that you lack the willpower to quit smoking, then you haven't yet understood the nature of the trap you're in. The more you will yourself to quit, the more you build up the belief that you're depriving yourself of something precious, and so the more you crave the very thing you're trying to give up.

This is how the rope tightens, keeping you firmly imprisoned. The only way to break the bonds is to understand the nature of the nicotine trap, let go of the struggle and unravel the brainwashing.

In other words:

YOU DON'T NEED WILLPOWER, YOU JUST NEED TO KILL THE BIG MONSTER

HOW WEAK-WILLED ARE YOU?

If you have tried and failed to quit in the past, did you put it down to a lack of willpower? Because the willpower method is so widely promoted, smokers don't question the validity behind it. You just assume that your failure to quit must be a flaw in yourself rather than the method. Believe me:

TELLING SOMEONE TO QUIT WITH THE WILLPOWER METHOD IS LIKE TELLING THEM TO OPEN A DOOR BY PUSHING ON THE HINGES

Ask yourself whether you're weak-willed in other ways. Perhaps you drink or eat too much and you regard this as further evidence of a weak will. There is a connection between all addictions, but it's not that they are signs of a lack of willpower. On the contrary, they are more likely evidence of a strong will. What they all share is that they are traps created by misleading information and untruths. And one of the most misleading untruths is that quitting requires willpower.

You have made up your mind to read a book called *Boot Camp* and do something to tackle your addiction. That doesn't sound like the act of a weak-willed person. In fact, most smokers are stubbornly strong-willed. It takes a strong-willed person to persist in doing something that goes against all their instincts. You know that smoking is dragging you further and further into the pit, making you increasingly stressed and unhappy, threatening to destroy your life, and yet you continue to do it.

The biggest fear for any drug addict is running out of their supply of the drug. Smokers go to incredible lengths to make sure they have a supply of cigarettes at all times. This requires tremendous organization, forethought and determination. Drug addicts are also determined liars. They will go way beyond the point of reason to deny their smoking to others and to themselves.

It also takes a strong will to persist in following a method that patently doesn't work. If I saw you trying to open a door by pushing on the hinges and I told you you'd find it easier if you pushed on the handle, but you ignored me and insisted on pushing on the hinges, I'd call you wilful, not weak-willed.

Think of all the people you know who are smokers. There are enough smokers in positions of power to illustrate that smoking is not exclusive to the weak-willed. World leaders, captains of industry, entertainers, doctors… we have more people from the medical profession coming to Easyway for help than from any other walk of life. All of them reached their position in life through determination and hard work. In other words, they have immense willpower. So why would their willpower fail them when they try to stop doing something that's destroying their health?

In fact, it tends to be the most strong-willed people who find it hardest to quit by using the willpower method. Why? Because when the door fails to open, they won't give up and try to find an easier method; they'll force themselves to keep pushing on the hinges until they can push no more.

◇◇

Exercise: **TIME FOR YOUR CIGARETTE OR E-CIGARETTE**

OK, it's time for your next cigarette. Not for any good reason – only that I've told you to keep smoking as you read the book so I think you should. So, are you going to do it or not?

A lot of people who come to Easyway take this instruction to keep smoking as their cue to stop. Smokers don't like being told what to do and just as they don't like being told when they can't smoke, they don't like being told when they can either.

Smokers like to tell themselves that they're in control of their smoking and one way of doing this is to choose when you smoke. It is only the illusion of control, but smokers cling on to it stubbornly. Anyway, carry on smoking or vaping as normal for the time being.

◇◇

BEWARE OTHER QUITTERS

People who try to quit by the willpower method can have a harmful effect on your own desire to quit. They either brag about the sacrifices they're making or they whine about them. Either way, they reinforce the false belief that quitting demands a sacrifice.

The braggers are easy to spot. They're the ones who become holier than thou anti-smoking zealots the moment they stub out what they hope will be their final cigarette. Up go the No Smoking signs in their homes and cars. They'll invite you round just so they can forbid you to smoke. And gloat.

They will take great delight in reminding you that by smoking you are ruining your health and burning a fortune and they will tell you how they find it incomprehensible that an intelligent person like you still finds reasons to put those filthy things in your mouth and set light to them. Of course, they've conveniently forgotten that they spent years doing the very same thing.

Ex-smokers who have quit through willpower are far more vitriolic in their attacks on smoking than people who have never smoked. Why are they so angry? Because beneath all the bragging and bluster they have not overcome their addiction. They still believe they've made a sacrifice and they resent anyone who continues to feed their addiction.

Beware of the braggers; they can have a very negative effect on smokers who are thinking of quitting. Their bullying can drive you into the arms of your little crutch and make you lose sight of the real enemy. But worse than that, they reinforce the belief that "Once a smoker, always a smoker". It's obvious that they still crave cigarettes so they create the impression that you can stop smoking but you can't escape.

This impression is confirmed by the whiners. Whiners will be the first to congratulate you when you smoke your last cigarette and throw the rest in the fire at midnight on New Year's Eve. They will shake your hand, wish you success, fuel your elation by telling you how much healthier and wealthier you'll be, that you've made a really important decision and will never regret it... and then bring you crashing down by telling you how they quit years ago but still miss it terribly on occasions like this.

It can be enough to send you scrambling to rescue your cigarettes from the fire and sneaking outside to light up while everyone else celebrates.

The last thing you want to hear when you're trying to quit is that you'll still be craving cigarettes years from now. The good news is you won't. Braggers and whiners only continue to crave cigarettes because they haven't killed the Big Monster. They have followed the wrong method and so they have nothing to offer you from their experience.

FIFTH INSTRUCTION: IGNORE ANY ADVICE
THAT GOES AGAINST EASYWAY

In particular, ignore the advice of anyone who claims to have quit by the willpower method. The fact is there is no sacrifice. The cigarette is NOT your friend so you are not "giving up" anything.

People who quit with the willpower method are always waiting for the moment when the struggle ends and they become a happy non-smoker. But because the Big Monster is still alive, there is no finish line, no point in time when they stop wishing they could smoke.

CROSSING THE LINE THE EASY WAY

With Easyway, there is nothing to wait for. You become a happy non-smoker the moment you unravel all the illusions that have led you into the nicotine trap, free yourself from fear and stop smoking with a feeling of excitement and elation. The elation of crossing the finish line occurs as soon as you remove the fear and illusions and stop smoking. That's when you kill the Big Monster and walk free from the addiction that has kept you enslaved. You need to understand that you will NOT get to that line by forcing yourself to suffer.

The psychology of the addict is such that a hard-line approach will not work. Rather than helping you to quit, it actually encourages you to stay hooked because:

1. It reinforces the myth that quitting is hard and, therefore, adds to your fear.

2. It creates a feeling of deprivation, which you will seek to alleviate in your usual way – you will fall back into the trap.

You only need willpower if you have a conflict of will. We are going to resolve that conflict by removing one side of the tug-of-war of fear, so that all your will is going against smoking. Using willpower for the rest of your life to try not to smoke is unlikely to prove successful and will not make you happy; removing the need and desire to smoke will.

ADDICTIVE PERSONALITY THEORY

THE ADDICTIVE PERSONALITY THEORY IS JUST THAT – A THEORY. THE BELIEF THAT SOME PEOPLE ARE MORE PRONE TO ADDICTION THAN OTHERS BECAUSE OF THE WAY THEY'RE MADE STEMS FROM LOOKING AT THE SITUATION FROM THE WRONG PERSPECTIVE. THE TRAITS SHARED BY ADDICTS ARE NOT THE CAUSE OF THEIR ADDICTION; THEY ARE THE RESULT.

A CONVENIENT EXCUSE

We're all agreed that there is a complete absence of logic in filling your lungs with poisonous fumes. This is why smokers are constantly making feeble excuses to justify why they do it:

"It helps me relax."

"I've got a lot of stress at the moment. I'll stop when things get easier."

"It's my life. I'm allowed one little indulgence."

We've established that all these excuses are founded on the myth that smoking provides some sort of pleasure or crutch. But even when all the usual excuses have been shot down in flames and it's pointed out that their real reason for smoking is nicotine addiction, there is one last desperate plea that some smokers fall back on to justify their decision not to tackle their addiction.

"I HAVE AN ADDICTIVE PERSONALITY."

They've been led to believe that there's something in their genetic make-up that makes them more susceptible than most people to becoming hooked, and this makes it harder for them to escape. Of course, it suits them to believe this. It's a convenient excuse, but not one that will do them any good. Believe in the theory of the addictive personality and all you do is ensure that you remain forever trapped.

Sadly, their misconception is backed up by a number of so-called "experts", who support the theory of the addictive personality. The term is bandied about so often that it's easy to be fooled into believing it's an established condition. It is not. It's a theory, largely based on the fact that a number of addicts are addicted to more than one thing, e.g. drinkers who are also smokers or gamblers, or heroin addicts who smoke and are heavily in debt.

But all addictions involve the same kind of trap, so it's obvious that someone who is susceptible to one addiction will be susceptible to others. It's nothing to do with genetics; it's all to do with not understanding the trap and believing the myth that these things give you a genuine pleasure or crutch. Remember,

THE MISERY OF ADDICTION IS NOT RELIEVED BY THE THING YOU ARE ADDICTED TO; IT'S CAUSED BY IT

SMOKERS WHO FAIL TO ESCAPE

The fear of success drives smokers to seek reasons to avoid even trying to quit. The addictive personality theory gives them the perfect excuse. If you think you have an addictive personality, you will regard quitting as an impossible task. "How can I override my own genetic make-up?" This illusion can also be reinforced by your failed attempts to quit by using willpower.

It is further confirmed by people who have quit by using the willpower method and are feeling deprived because they still believe they're making a sacrifice – the braggers and whiners we covered earlier. If they've abstained for years and are still craving their little crutch, and we've established that it's nothing to do with willpower, it's tempting to believe that there must be some flaw in their genetic make-up that keeps drawing them back.

But there is another explanation.

THEY'VE BEEN CONNED

Braggers and whiners are still labouring under the illusion that they are making a genuine sacrifice. Their willpower is pulling them in opposite directions: they desperately want to satisfy their craving, yet they desperately want to be a non-smoker too. They are caught up in the tug-of-war of fear and eventually they lose – all because of an illusion.

We've established that you are not "giving up" anything. This gives you an enormous advantage over the braggers and whiners. Make sure you're not fooled by the illusion that keeps them in the trap.

Pleading an addictive personality is just another excuse for doing something that you know is completely illogical. You don't want to stay enslaved by the Big Monster, with all the fear, misery and sickness that goes with it. That's why you're reading this book. You have made the decision to escape and you are well on the way to doing just that.

Escape is easy, provided you keep an open mind. If you cling to the excuse that you have an addictive personality, it means that your mind is not open and you risk sentencing yourself to remain enslaved for the rest of your life.

When you keep trying and failing to quit you end up feeling stupid and helpless. Putting your addiction down to a flaw in your personality can appear to be the rational explanation you need. With Easyway, you discover the real explanation. The spread of misinformation is so relentless that anybody can be conned, and most people are to some extent, even non-smokers. You weren't stupid to get hooked and neither were the millions of other smokers. Neither are you stupid or weak for being unable to quit. You've just been following the wrong method.

Once you see the true picture of how addiction works, the illusions disappear and you realize that you are complete without your little crutch. With it, you are a slave.

DEGREES OF ADDICTION

So why do some people fall deeper into the trap than others? Why can one person have the occasional cigarette, while another ends up puffing their way through 60 a day? Doesn't that suggest that one is more prone to addiction than the other?

Well, yes, it does, but why should that have anything to do with their personality? There are numerous differences between people, which can explain why one is prone to smoking more than another. All the people who are reading this book right now will smoke different amounts due to different circumstances, such as money and opportunity, but all of you feel the same way about smoking and are trying to find the same solution.

The first experience of smoking is revolting. For some people, that's enough to put them off ever smoking again. Others see it as a challenge that must be surmounted if they are to earn respect, and make a point of smoking as much as they can.

Others can't afford to smoke more than a few cigarettes a day.

Our behaviour is largely affected by the influences we are subjected to as we grow up: different parents, teachers, friends, things we read, watch and listen to, places we go, people we meet, etc. All these factors will have a bearing on how quickly we descend into the trap and they vary for everybody. But they are all controllable and reversible. They have nothing to do with genetics or anything fixed in our personality. Be quite clear:

ANYBODY CAN FALL INTO THE SMOKING TRAP

AND ANYBODY CAN ESCAPE JUST AS EASILY

LIES, DAMNED LIES AND STATISTICS

Addiction is a lonely place. Despite the knowledge that millions of people in the world are suffering with the same addiction, smokers, drinkers and other addicts all think that their own problem is unique to them. When you come out of your cocoon and speak to people about your problems and discover that they are experiencing, or have experienced, exactly what you are going through, then you begin to see that addiction is not a weakness in the individual, but a weakness in the society that brainwashes individuals into the trap.

Next time you have to go outside to smoke, pay attention to the other smokers out there with you. Birds of a feather flock together and smokers certainly appear to be flocking when you see them huddled together in the rain outside their workplaces, "enjoying" a cigarette. As a smoker there is a sense that you're a different breed from everyone else. You appear to share similar character traits and you feel more comfortable in their company.

The temptation is to believe that these traits are evidence of a shared personality – an addictive personality that led you to become a smoker. The reality is that they are the *result* of smoking.

The reason addicts feel more comfortable in the company of similar addicts is not because they're more interesting or fun; on the contrary, the attraction lies in the very fact that they won't challenge you or make you think twice about your addiction because they're in the same boat. All addicts know that they're doing something stupid and self-destructive. If you're surrounded by other people doing the same thing, you don't feel quite so foolish.

The good news is that, once you're free from the addiction, you also get free from the harmful effects it has on your character.

The belief that you were doomed from birth to be a smoker will be self-fulfilling if you allow it to remain in your mind. Think about it logically. The addictive personality theory is based on statistics, but if you examine the statistics closely they actually make the likelihood of an addictive gene appear far-fetched.

If there was an addictive gene, you would expect the percentage of addicts in the world to have remained fairly constant throughout history. Yet in less than a century, the incidence of nicotine addiction has changed dramatically. In the 1940s more than 80 per cent of the UK adult male population were smokers; today it's less than 20 per cent. A similar trend is evident throughout most of Western Europe and North America. So are we to conclude that the proportion of people with addictive personalities has fallen by 55 per cent in just over half a century? That's a major genetic shift in mankind!

At the same time, the number of smokers in Asia has soared. What complex genetic anomaly is this that rises and falls so rapidly, and even appears to transfer itself wholesale from one continent to another?

It doesn't really matter if you believe you have an addictive personality or gene anyway – the fact is that it is easy to get free just as long as you know how, regardless of whether you have an addictive personality or gene or not.

EFFECT NOT CAUSE

It's essential that you understand that you didn't become addicted to nicotine because you have an addictive personality. If you think you have an addictive personality, it's simply because you got addicted to nicotine.

This is the trick that addiction plays on you. It makes you feel that you're dependent on your addiction and that there's some weakness in your character or genetic make-up. It distorts your perceptions and thereby maintains its grip on you.

The addictive personality theory encourages the belief that escape is out of your hands and that you are condemned to a life of slavery and misery. Remember, you didn't feel the need or desire to smoke until you started smoking. It was smoking that created the addiction, not the other way around.

On Day Four, the misery and slavery of nicotine addiction will be behind you. Once you have stripped away all the illusions and can see the situation in its true light without any doubts whatsoever, you'll wonder how you were ever conned into seeing it differently. But like millions of people around the world, you have been the victim of an ingenious trap. Recognize the trap for what it is, dismiss the idea of a flaw in your personality and you will be ready to walk free.

Just keep an open mind and keep following all the instructions.

CONQUERING CONCENTRATION

THE IMAGE OF SHERLOCK HOLMES PUFFING AWAY ON HIS PIPE AS HE TRIES TO CRACK HIS LATEST CASE HAS BECOME A SYMBOL FOR ANOTHER OF THE GREAT MYTHS: THAT SMOKING HELPS YOU CONCENTRATE. IT'S ESSENTIAL THAT YOU REMOVE THIS BELIEF FROM YOUR MIND BEFORE YOU QUIT. IT'S EMBARRASSING IN OUR LIVE SEMINARS WHEN A SMOKER CITES SHERLOCK AS AN EXAMPLE OF AN INTELLECTUAL HIGH ACHIEVER WHO SMOKED. IT NEVER OCCURS TO THEM, UNTIL WE GENTLY POINT IT OUT, THAT OF COURSE HOLMES IS AN ENTIRELY FICTIONAL CHARACTER.

A BRAINWASHED BELIEF

Up until now you have been encouraged not to change your normal smoking pattern because we don't want you to suffer any distractions while you're reading the book. You may have interpreted this to mean that continuing to smoke will help you concentrate. Believe me, it means nothing of the sort.

SMOKING DESTROYS CONCENTRATION

Smokers are brainwashed into believing that smoking aids concentration and the back-to-front nature of the trap appears to confirm the fact.

Until you remove this belief from your mind, you will find it hard to concentrate if you're craving a cigarette. So have a cigarette when you feel the craving and continue to read the book without distractions.

We all have times, whether in our work or our home life, when we need to focus on a problem and we don't relish the thought. For smokers, this is a common trigger for reaching for a cigarette. You believe that smoking can do two things: relieve the anxiety of confronting the problem and help you to rally your thoughts into finding a solution. As soon as this belief is planted in your mind, it becomes impossible to concentrate. No matter how hard you try to concentrate on the problem, the thought that a cigarette will make the situation better becomes an increasing distraction.

Eventually you cave in and light up a cigarette. The anxiety disappears and you find the answer you've been looking for. Naturally you conclude that the cigarette has made all the difference. You needed the cigarette to be able to concentrate.

So far so predictable.

You believed a cigarette would help you concentrate.

You smoked a cigarette.

You found the concentration you needed…

What's the problem?

The problem is that it's an illusion – one that's keeping you in the nicotine trap, choking yourself to death and burning your money.

So what really happened?

You believed a cigarette would help you concentrate.

You became obsessed with the idea, so you were unable to concentrate until you smoked.

The cigarette appeared to solve the problem but it actually caused it. It's like someone stealing the tiles off your roof and then coming around and offering to sell them back to you the very next day.

Exercise: **DRIVEN TO DISTRACTION**

The ability to concentrate means removing all distractions, so let's investigate just how distracting your smoking experience is. Have a cigarette now and take note of all the different steps you have to go through. You have to find your packet, take the cigarette out, light it, inhale the fumes, exhale them, flick the ash into the ashtray. You have to repeat this about 20 times for each cigarette, then put it out, empty the ashtray, take out another one, light it and repeat the whole process again and again.

Non-smokers don't have any of these distractions when they have a problem to solve. Neither do they suffer the distraction of craving the cigarette in the first place, a craving that is only partially relieved by the cigarette. And neither do they starve their brain of oxygen, as you do every time you smoke, so their ability to think clearly and creatively is not hampered.

Not only does smoking create countless distractions, it also destroys your ability to concentrate.

NO OPTION, NO DISTRACTION

When we're faced with a problem we don't like, we seek comfort in distractions because they delay the dreaded moment when we have to get to grips with the problem. Some people make a cup of tea, some make themselves something to eat, some check their emails or look at their phone. We convince ourselves that there's value in doing these things because that gives us the excuse to put off the inevitable.

But none of these things help to solve the problem. In fact, they only make it worse. Leave a problem unsolved and it will usually get bigger. It certainly won't go away. But as long as we have the belief that any of these things will help, we won't be able to tackle the problem properly until we do them. Smoking is just another self-imposed distraction. It's not the physical craving for a cigarette that prevents us from being able to concentrate, because that craving is almost indiscernible. It's the mental obsession caused by the Big Monster.

You can prove your own ability to concentrate without cigarettes by putting yourself in a situation where smoking is not an option. A good example is an exam room. Every year countless students sit their finals. A proportion of them are smokers, who are used to studying with a cigarette on the go. When it dawns on them that they are going to have to sit through hours in an exam room without smoking, panic sets in. They try sitting a practice paper without smoking and find their hands shaking so much they can't write!

Yet when it comes to the exam proper, they sit through it without the thought of smoking ever entering their heads. It's clear that they are perfectly capable of concentrating for several hours without their little crutch.

So what makes all the difference? Quite simply the fact that smoking was never an option in the exam room, so it never became a distraction.

When you know you can't have something it's easy to put it out of your mind. Millions of smokers have discovered this since smoking was banned on planes and trains. What would once have been a dreaded situation is no problem at all because they don't spend the journey moping for something they can't have. They can put the thought out of their mind until they reach their destination.

Actually, let me digress for a few moments here, because I'd like to recap on how weak nicotine addiction is and there's a great example involving a smoker on a flight that illustrates it perfectly.

Consider a heavy smoker on a long-haul flight who cannot smoke.

He resigns herself to this fact. Most smokers – even the heaviest in these circumstances – don't even bother using nicotine patches or gum.

For most of the flight, they feel calm. Yet, 10 hours into an 11-hour flight, something begins to happen. The flight is coming to an end and the smoker begins to anticipate getting off the plane and being able to light up a cigarette.

As the smoker checks his watch and notes there is now only the small matter of 20 minutes until the end of the flight, he smiles.

Now imagine that smoker when the flight's captain announces that he is very sorry, but due to severe weather conditions at their destination, the flight has been diverted to a different airport and the flight will now last a further 60 minutes.

Wow! All of a sudden, the calm disappears, along with the smile, from the smoker's face as he lurches into a condition that he would immediately describe as nicotine withdrawal: anger, tension, anxiety, upset, and stress.

Nicotine withdrawal didn't just happen in the six seconds that it took the pilot to announce the delayed landing. It has been occurring continuously since the smoker stubbed out his cigarette before he boarded the flight more than 10 hours and 40 minutes ago.

But nicotine withdrawal did not cause the sudden onset of unpleasant symptoms.

Something in the smoker's mind changed as a result of the pilot's announcement: it was the Big Monster.

John's Nicotine Withdrawal Story

Former chain-smoker, cured by Allen Carr, John Dicey, Global CEO
& Senior Therapist, Allen Carr's Easyway

I remember very clearly as a smoker, when I used to go to parties, particularly the wild ones of my youth, I'd take at least three packs of cigarettes with me.

Now, I was a chain-smoker, but not even I would need 60 cigarettes for a few hours at a party. So why did I take so many?

Well, at parties you have these terrible people who only smoke other people's cigarettes. Maybe you're one of them… if so, I mean no offence, but for a chain-smoker such people are to be feared more than any drunken bore.

That's because they have a tendency to smoke "real smokers'" cigarettes, never buying their own, not even when they know they will be smoking at a party. It's not the cost of the cigarettes that upsets chain-smokers; it's the fact that these so-called "social smokers" deplete their evening's supply of cigarettes… that's why the chain-smoker will always think ahead and take extra.

Probably even worse are the "light smokers", the kind that don't mind if they run through their personal supply of cigarettes at the party knowing they'll almost certainly be able to smoke someone else's. They don't care about exhausting that person's supplies.

And have you noticed that even casual or light smokers tend to become chain-smokers at parties? Eventually, these part-time smokers leave the poor "real smoker" short of cigarettes at the end of the evening when the shops are closed. It's a chain-smoker's nightmare. It was for this very reason that I always carried several packs secreted in my jacket pockets.

But I recall one party when I suffered a terrible blow. Having left my extra packs of cigarettes in my jacket, which had been stolen during the party, I arrived home and absent-mindedly reached into my pocket for my only remaining packet.

It was like being struck by lightning when I noticed the first tell-tale sign: the pack was TOO light – not heavy enough to contain many cigarettes. There was a soft rattle as I shook the pack. My heart seemed to stop; my pulse was racing. Fear! Anxiety! Stress! Panic! It was the dire feeling that I once used to mistake for the physical symptoms of nicotine withdrawal.

I could hardly bear to open the packet. I knew it wasn't going to be good news. I looked inside. There were just TWO cigarettes.

My feelings of panic got worse.

If you're a heavy smoker, you'll understand exactly what I'm talking about. It's the feeling we think of as the physical need for nicotine. Yet it appeared in a matter of seconds when I felt the lightness of the cigarette pack.

Where had it been a few seconds before?

What's more, I was so panicked I immediately lit one of the cigarettes. NOW I ONLY HAD ONE CIGARETTE left. And the physical feeling was actually getting worse.

Consider the fact that my body was flooded with nicotine; it was rushing into my body faster than heroin does when injected into a vein – yet somehow, I was experiencing a feeling I identified at the time as physical withdrawal from nicotine.

There was no withdrawal though. Nicotine was on its way INTO my body. I was smoking! Whatever was happening couldn't possibly have been nicotine withdrawal.

I was experiencing real physical feelings, but they were purely the result of a mental process. A thought process created those feelings – not withdrawal from the drug. Something in my mind changed as a result of the cigarette shortage.

Now, if you follow what I have said, I hope that this reminds you that nicotine withdrawal doesn't cause the really unpleasant symptoms. They originate in the mind courtesy of the Big Monster, and Boot Camp will kill them.

IT'S NOT A WEIGHTY MATTER

One of the most common misconceptions about smoking is that it plays a part in helping to control weight.

There are several factors involved in this illusion: the belief that smoking acts as an appetite suppressant enabling smokers to skip meals and snacks (substituting food for cigarettes); the idea that smoking burns calories by increasing the smoker's metabolic rate; and the relentless influence of the tobacco industry, which continues the work it started years ago, portraying glamorous svelte stars of the silver screen with cigarettes permanently attached to their fingers and lips – Big Tobacco has infiltrated the fashion and music industries and continues to manipulate the movie industry.

Young bands, solo performers, and sports stars continue to have their images used in adverts and sponsorship tours across the globe. And in countries where advertising is banned, they influence the inclusion of smoking in photo-shoots, and paparazzi shots in newspapers. The fashion industry is the most blatant in its cosy arrangements with the tobacco giants, with cigarettes frequently appearing on the fashion show runways and in glossy shoots for magazines.

Hollywood is always eager to assist too. There are many examples of leading characters being portrayed as smokers, bizarrely, even in movies set hundreds of years into the future. It's always the same message: smoking is cool, smoking is tough and, even more important, smoking will survive.

No wonder by the time a potential smoker reaches an age whereby they might be tempted to smoke, they're already convinced that it's a cool, sophisticated, stylish, sexy thing to do, with the added benefit that it's also some kind of magical means of controlling weight.

You're not an idiot; you don't need me to tell you that those sexy, glamorous, stylish and sophisticated stars weren't made to look that way by cigarettes. It was the other way around: the stars made cigarettes appear sexy, glamorous, stylish, and sophisticated. Cigarettes just aren't sexy!

The same goes for the myth of the smoking rebel. There are a million ways of rebelling, none of which involve being a pathetic victim of an awful addiction. You choose to rebel; you don't choose whether you smoke or not. There is truly nothing sadder than a smoker who claims they're doing it for this reason – deep down inside, not even they believe it. They know that, far from smoking being rebellious, they're smoking because they're enslaved.

So what about the weight issue? Firstly, you know yourself, you see plenty of overweight smokers. If smoking was that efficient, surely that wouldn't be the case. More importantly, if that was the case, the more someone smoked, the skinnier they'd be – but chain-smokers tend to be the most overweight of all.

Smoking does indeed increase your metabolic rate, the rate at which your body burns calories. Glossy fitness magazines hark on endlessly about this. What they don't tell their readers is that the impact of smoking on your metabolic rate is insignificant in terms of weight control. Think how hard and long you have to pedal on an exercise bike at the gym to burn off a few hundred calories. There simply isn't this fat-burning, calorie-burning process going on in your body as a result of your smoking.

Another favourite myth of glossy magazines is that smoking acts as an appetite suppressant. It seems to make sense to us as smokers. We get hungry, have a cigarette, and the hunger goes. In our mind it's the cigarette that's magically taken away our hunger. What we don't realize is that, when a non-smoker ignores hunger for a couple of minutes, their hunger also disappears. Non-smokers don't give the credit for this to cigarettes; but for smokers, it confirms the myth that smoking suppresses appetite. They ignore the fact that, when they experience more severe hunger, a cigarette won't do the trick. And it never did.

Pick up your pack of cigarettes. Examine the pack carefully. Can you find the text that says, "Used as part of a calorie controlled diet these cigarettes will help you control weight"? Of course, nothing of the sort is written on the pack. Why not? Because it's not true. If it was, the tobacco companies would be allowed to write it on the packet and no one could stop them.

So how have we become so convinced that smoking helps with weight control? It's our, and others, failed attempts to quit smoking using willpower that causes the problem. If it hasn't happened to you, it will have happened to someone you know. Smokers quit smoking and put on weight. Why? They haven't killed the Big Monster and therefore constantly feel deprived.

In an attempt to get rid of the desire to smoke and feeling of deprivation they tend to eat or drink in place of smoking. It doesn't really work, but nevertheless they carry on and gain weight as a result. When they finally cave in and smoke again, they stop overeating and the weight seems to drop off. It confirms the myth, meaning the fear of gaining weight stays with them and puts them off ever trying to quit smoking again.

This doesn't happen with Easyway. Why not? Because Easyway removes the desire to smoke. If there is no desire to smoke there is no feeling of deprivation, and there is no need or compulsion to substitute (eat or drink instead of smoke).

You won't be inclined to substitute when you quit smoking with Easyway, so there is no need for you to gain weight. Far from it, you'll be so full of energy you'll be glowing with good health.

I'll talk more about the link between smoking and hunger later, but for the time being, if you're concerned about weight gain, rest assured it simply isn't going to happen this time.

You won't cure a weight problem by smoking; neither will you cause one when you use Easyway.

DEPRESSION AND SELF-HARM

We receive letters and emails every week from smokers all over the world asking for clarification on certain points.

Be reassured that as a result of all this correspondence, you hold in your hands the most up-to-date and comprehensive version of the written method to date.

Two issues that arise with a small number of correspondents are those relating to acute/chronic depression and self-harm. These are two quite separate issues; nevertheless, I'm happy to handle them in the same section. Smokers who live with those conditions are concerned that Easyway may not work for them. Those suffering with severe depression sense that smoking helps them deal with the problem in some way. In fact, it's quite the reverse. Smoking has been proven to cause and exacerbate depression rather than ease it, so please rest assured, if you live with that extremely challenging condition, the Easyway Boot Camp will still work for you. Any belief that smoking helps you deal with your depression is understandable but no different from any smoker who believes, for example, that smoking helps them cope with stress. You can relate to every part of the method and the way we're fooled into believing that smoking helps us cope with depression is exactly the same as with stress.

As far as self-harm is concerned, a smoker might say something to the effect of "I smoke to punish myself or hurt myself or because I don't care about myself." If you harbour those beliefs, you need to understand that you don't smoke because it harms you; you smoke because you are addicted to nicotine. On some level, you may be choosing to self-harm, yet you have no choice as to whether you smoke or not. In this way, you're no different from any smoker on this planet.

Self-harm may well have been the motivation to start smoking, but remember we all started smoking for a variety of phoney and foolish reasons; whether it was to be part of the gang, or the opposite, to go against the flow and rebel, or to try to look tough, cool or sophisticated, or just out of sheer curiosity, or just to show the world that we didn't care. The fact is that the reason we start smoking has no bearing on why we then continue to smoke, nor does it prevent us from stopping.

There are many more effective, efficient, and significant ways that you might be able to self-harm if that is what you wish to do. Smoking is entirely unsatisfactory in that regard since it takes years, sometimes decades, to get what might be described as the self-harm pay-off.

People who want to self-harm do it immediately and painfully. Put simply, self-harm isn't why you smoke.

It might be one of the reasons you lit your first cigarette, and it might be an excuse you use to justify the fact that you have carried on smoking or to excuse yourself for your failure to quit, but it simply is not why you smoke. To claim otherwise implies that you have some kind of choice or control over smoking. If you had any choice over whether you smoke or not, you wouldn't be reading this book. Don't get me wrong, perhaps in the past, when you fell back into smoking, after a period of freedom, you did so with an attitude of "So what – I don't care if I live or die!" but at that point you didn't throw yourself off a cliff. In that situation, it's no more than a phoney justification for returning to smoking. The real reason for the return to smoking was the belief that smoking does something for you.

The great news is that, because self-harm isn't why you've been smoking, you have no need to swap smoking as a means of hurting yourself for any other self-harming activity once you've quit. People who live with depression and genuine self-harming issues do so with amazing strength and resilience and deserve our respect and admiration for doing so. The wonderful news is that, no matter what highs or lows might befall you once you've quit, I can assure you that the highs will be higher and the lows will be less intense and easier to handle.

HOW TO CONCENTRATE

The first thing you need to do in order to concentrate on anything is remove all distractions. If someone's making a distracting noise you can ask them to stop or you can move to somewhere quiet. But say you're the one causing the distraction – perhaps you have a cold and are constantly sniffing – it's a distraction, but what can you do about it? Nothing, so you just put it out of your mind and focus on the job in hand.

If there is something you can do to remove a distraction, you need to do it or else it will irritate you and that will become an added distraction. If there is nothing you can do about it, it's much easier to ignore it and put it out of your mind. When you have a choice, you have to make a decision. Until you make that decision, you will be distracted by the choice. Take away the choice and you take away the pressure to make a decision.

Perhaps you think I'm suggesting that enforced denial is the key to quitting smoking permanently. Absolutely not. But the way smokers are able to get by quite happily when smoking is not an option does prove that it's easy to put smoking out of your mind, even when you're still hooked.

The problem for smokers and vapers is that the option to smoke is available most of the time. When you try to quit with the willpower method, you are always aware of that option and always distracted by it. With Easyway, you remove the option to smoke, not by denying yourself cigarettes but by removing all desire to smoke or vape.

For non-smokers, smoking is never a serious option and it won't be for you when you reach the end of this book.

BORING BORING SMOKING

Closely associated with the concentration myth is the myth that smoking helps to alleviate boredom. Again, this myth is created by the back-to-front nature of the trap. When your brain is not stimulated you have nothing to take your mind off the cries of the Little Monster, and so you tend to scratch the itch.

Smoking becomes your default response to boredom. But it doesn't remove the boredom.

Boredom is relieved by occupying your mind with something interesting. The exam room scenario proves that smokers can go for long periods without a cigarette and not even notice it when their minds are occupied. But there's nothing interesting about smoking a cigarette. When you're taking a drag of that toxic smoke, are you really thinking, "This cigarette is fascinating!" There are few more tediously repetitive activities than smoking a cigarette, again and again, day in, day out. It may be a fascination at the very beginning, but it quickly becomes so boring that you're not even aware of most of the cigarettes you smoke.

Take a close look at smokers next time you're stuck in traffic. They'll have a cigarette on the go, but they'll be every bit as bored as everyone else in the jam. Look at the smokers huddled outside work taking one of their cigarette breaks. Do they look stimulated and happy? Or do they look bored and miserable?

Just as smoking destroys concentration, it also increases boredom by reducing your opportunities for physical and mental stimulation, depleting your energy, making you sluggish, lethargic and lazy and destroying your zest for life.

FREEDOM FROM BRAINWASHING

Nicotine addiction is a tyrant. Just when you think you're putting up a resistance to the desire to smoke, something comes along that triggers the belief that you "need" a cigarette and all your resistance crumbles. A typical trigger is a problem that demands your attention. Up go your stress levels and, because you've been brainwashed into believing that smoking relieves stress, you reach for a cigarette.

So how can you avoid these triggers after you quit? Simple:

YOU DON'T NEED TO AVOID THE TRIGGERS

When you understand how the triggers work, they cease to be triggers. Everybody comes up against tricky problems from time to time. It's a fact of life. But not everybody reaches for a cigarette every time they're faced with a problem that demands concentration. Non-smokers don't see cigarettes as a crutch that will help them cope with the challenge and consequently they spend much less time agonizing over problems.

The problem smokers have is that, in addition to the real-life problem that's facing them, they have the uncertainty about whether or not they should smoke. So they have not one difficult decision to make but two. This delays the process of tackling the real problem, dragging it out and making it worse while they try to cope with the distraction of the cigarette.

REMOVE THE DOUBT FROM A SMOKER'S MIND AND QUITTING BECOMES EASY

There may come a time after you've smoked your final cigarette when you find yourself faced with a stressful problem and the thought enters your head to light up a cigarette. It's important that you prepare yourself for this and are not alarmed. The thought is just a hangover from your smoking days. You don't have to go along with it. All you have to do is remind yourself of what you know to be the truth: smoking benefits you in no way whatsoever; you know you've made the right decision; and no purpose will be served by delving into the subject.

Instead of feeling deprived, rejoice in the fact that you are now a non-smoker and you have no need to fall into the tyrant's trap.

People who quit with the willpower method spend the rest of their lives trying to avoid the triggers that used to make them reach for a cigarette. They don't trust themselves to resist the temptation to smoke if any of those triggers occur. When you have the certainty that smoking does absolutely nothing for you whatsoever, there is no need to avoid the triggers because they no longer work as triggers.

Indeed, the triggers can serve to reinforce your sense of satisfaction and joy at having quit. Every time something happens that reminds you of when you used to smoke, enjoy the reminder that you are free.

ACHIEVING CERTAINTY

Removing the doubt and achieving the certainty you need is a simple process of looking at the facts and seeing things as they really are. Most smokers don't do this when they try to quit. They just look at the reasons for not smoking – the health risks, the wasted money, the smell, etc. – and hope that will be enough to overcome their desire to smoke.

Of course, the Big Monster isn't going to be silenced by such concerns. If it was, no smoker would have any trouble quitting. In order to kill the Big Monster, you need to see smoking for what it really is – a drug addiction that does nothing for you whatsoever – and allow understanding to replace brainwashing.

SIXTH INSTRUCTION: HAVE NO DOUBT ABOUT YOUR DECISION TO QUIT

When you are certain that smoking does nothing for you, you will find that your desire to smoke evaporates. The only reason anyone chooses to smoke is because of the myth that it provides some sort of pleasure or crutch. Unravel the myth and you remove the desire.

You are now halfway to achieving your dream of becoming free from nicotine, a happy non-smoker. I should add the word "again", because you were free from the tyranny of addiction before you started smoking. You may have forgotten what it felt like. After your final cigarette, you will quickly rediscover the pleasures and benefits of being a non-smoker.

Better health

More money

Greater self-esteem

In addition, you will discover the truth that has been hidden from you while you've been under the tyranny of nicotine addiction: that without cigarettes you will be:

More relaxed

More resilient to stress

Better able to concentrate

You will also enjoy all your meals more because your taste buds will regain their sensitivity and you'll be happy to take your time rather than rush to the end so you can smoke or vape. You will have the energy to get more out of exercise and sex. And best of all, you'll be free from the sense of slavery that leaves all smokers feeling helpless and stupid.

Tomorrow is a big day. It's the day you finish off the Big Monster. So enjoy the thought that you are taking steps to free yourself from the tyranny of nicotine addiction and sleep well tonight. And carry on smoking, vaping, or using whatever nicotine product you use. Don't feel guilty, don't be concerned about it – freedom awaits. All you need to do is follow the instructions.

CHECKLIST

I understand that:

○ I am not "giving up" anything.

○ No smoker has ever enjoyed smoking.

○ Quitting is only hard if you use the wrong method.

○ Willpower won't help me to quit – if anything it will make it harder.

○ People who brag or whine about quitting by willpower still believe they are making a sacrifice.

○ My addiction to nicotine is all to do with the drug and nothing to do with my personality.

○ Smoking, vaping and all nicotine products destroy concentration.

○ Smoking, vaping and all nicotine products do not help with weight control or appetite suppression, reduce depression or act as an expression of self-harm.

○ There is no need to avoid the triggers when you have no desire to smoke.

KILLING OFF THE BIG MONSTER

Today is a big day. We are going to deliver the final fatal blows to the Big Monster, free your mind from any lingering belief that smoking provides you with any kind of pleasure or crutch and snuff out your desire for a cigarette once and for all.

On the way, we will examine more of the myths that keep smokers in the trap, including the theory that substitutes can help you get through the process of quitting by keeping you topped up with nicotine while you work on getting out of "the habit". Remember, you don't smoke out of habit, you smoke because you're hooked on nicotine. Keep taking nicotine – in any form – and you're going to stay hooked.

A lot of people are drawn to smoking and a lot are therefore put off trying to quit, by the myth that smoking is a good way to keep your weight down.

We will look closely again at the connection between smoking and weight and explain why you will find it much easier to get in shape when you're not a slave to nicotine.

We will then look at the different types of smoker – the casual smokers, heavy smokers, stoppers and starters, etc. – and examine what, if anything, makes them different. You might be surprised by the conclusion. But if you're clear on everything you've read so far, you should already have guessed it.

By the end of these chapters, you will be ready and eager to stub out your final cigarette and get on with life as a happy non-smoker, but you might still have one or two burning questions that are making you feel uncertainty. We need to eradicate all uncertainty when it comes to your decision to quit. So we will address all the lingering doubts, so that tomorrow you are fully prepared to take that momentous step and walk free from the nicotine trap and smoke your final cigarette.

Congratulations on your achievements so far. You have come a very long way towards freeing yourself from the tyranny of smoking. Your mindset is already very different to how it was before you started the book. The myths that have kept you in the nicotine trap have started to unravel and you are moving closer and closer to destroying the Big Monster once and for all.

Perhaps you feel you have already destroyed it; in which case you're ahead of the game. That's great news but beware! Remember what I said about the instructions: you need to follow them all in order until the end. If you skip past any part of the book, you will not be following the method and you will miss out on a key step in your journey to freedom. This might not seem important now while you're full of zeal for quitting, but later you may be vulnerable to being dragged back into the trap if you don't follow the method in full.

So let's get on with Day Three. It begins with a close look at the way the Big Monster takes shape in your mind.

SPREADING THE MYTH

"It is perfectly possible for a man to be out of prison and yet not free – to be under no physical constraint and yet to be a psychological captive, compelled to think, feel and act as the representatives of the national State, or of some private interest within the nation, want him to think, feel and act."

Aldous Huxley, *Brave New World*

THE BIG CON

To use the words of Aldous Huxley, smokers, and in fact all nicotine addicts, are "psychological captives". Perhaps you think I'm going too far in comparing the world of nicotine addiction to the *Brave New World* of Huxley's imagination. OK, smoking is a killer and nicotine is a highly addictive drug, but surely I'm not suggesting that the tobacco industry and the pharmaceutical industry, with the nicotine industry carved up between them, are so evil as to trap their victims into a spiral of self-destruction by brainwashing them into believing its products are good for them, or at least not so bad for them!

Well, any industry that continues to push out products that are proven to be the cause of more than seven million deaths every year worldwide can hardly be held up as a paragon of virtue but there is something far more sinister at work. Even the tobacco industry is not clever enough to devise the level of brainwashing that leads millions of people to smoke themselves to death every year. It doesn't have to.

SMOKERS ARE ALREADY DOING THE INDUSTRY'S DIRTY WORK

Nobody spreads the myths that con us into smoking more than smokers themselves. It seems incredible, doesn't it? No smoker enjoys smoking, every smoker wishes they could stop, yet every smoker promotes the belief that smoking provides some kind of pleasure or crutch.

Exercise: **THE PRISON CAMP**

Imagine you've arrived at a prison camp in which millions of people have been imprisoned by a vicious tyrant. The conditions in this camp are terrible and all the prisoners are miserable. If they worked together, they could easily break down the walls that are keeping them captive, but the force that's keeping them imprisoned is incredibly powerful and they feel powerless to escape.

You discover that the tyrant keeps control of all the prisoners in the camp not by holding a gun to anybody's head but through cunning manipulation of their minds. Every prisoner is afraid of trying to escape because they've been warned that it will involve a terrible sacrifice and if they fail in their attempt, life inside the prison camp will get worse for them. They feel they are somehow being looked after while they're in the prison camp and they believe that life outside the camp will be unbearable.

They're so scared of the consequences of trying to

escape that they actually turn on anyone who tries to escape, rather than turning on their captor.

As you examine the prison camp more closely, you realize there is actually nothing keeping the prisoners in. There are no guards, no guns, no walls, no gates, nothing. You also know that life outside the prison camp is infinitely preferable to the life they're leading. They could walk out easily and instantly discover the joy of freedom. Yet their beliefs are keeping them captive. And together they have created a situation whereby everyone in the camp plays a part in keeping everyone imprisoned.

It's obvious to you what they need to do to escape this miserable situation:

STOP BEING CONNED BY THOSE FALSE BELIEFS

Your challenge is to find a way to show them the truth.

This scenario puts you in the position of a non-smoker, looking at smokers and wondering why they continue to punish themselves? This is the situation I found myself in when I had my moment of revelation and embarked on my mission to cure the world of smoking. The solution is simple – it's getting smokers to stop listening to each other and start hearing the truth about smoking that poses the challenge.

It's time for you to see the nicotine industry as it really is: an addiction business which is designed to enslave you for life. For life!!

You may be thinking that it's okay to call out the tobacco industry;

they've been proven not to care, but surely I shouldn't be so tough on the pharmaceutical industry. Don't they exist in order to do good? Aren't nicotine patches and gum and e-cigarettes the result of their desire to cure smokers of their addiction?

The pharmaceutical industry does an awful lot of good. But it also does tremendous harm. Their manipulation of clinical trials is well chronicled. And if you observe the nature of the beast, you'll notice they're incentivized to find treatments rather than cures – preferably treatments that last a lifetime. The reason is obvious. A lifetime of prescriptions and Big Pharma's coffers start overflowing. There is no better "medicine" in the pharmaceutical companies' eyes than one which is highly addictive and which has to be taken for life! No wonder the pharma industry and tobacco industry are becoming inseparable as they slice up the lucrative new e-cigarette market between themselves.

The discovery of the Easyway method has had an incredible impact on the smoking world and helped tens of millions of prisoners to get free, but countless millions still remain in the camp, trapped by their own false beliefs and the hugely powerful influence of other smokers.

GETTING HOOKED

The influence of other smokers is what lured you into the trap in the first place. In the vast majority of cases that first cigarette will have been provided by another smoker. It seemed like a generous and flattering gesture at the time. They probably offered you your second, too, and your third. As a novice smoker you might tell yourself you won't get hooked on it, you're just dabbling. The taste and smell are so foul you feel confident you could never get hooked on it, but before long you're buying your own.

You know you can't keep scrounging cigarettes off other people so eventually you take the plunge and pay for your own packet. You're eager to repay the debt so you start offering your cigarettes to the smokers who started you off with theirs, as well as any other smokers you come into contact with. Already you are helping to promote the myth.

But the influence of other smokers doesn't stop at offering you cigarettes. It is mostly responsible for your own decision to start smoking and for the myths that keep you in the nicotine trap.

Ask a smoker if they would recommend others to take up smoking and they are most likely to say, "No way!" Yet unwittingly they do just that. And it's often the people who care about you most that do the most damage. Parents who smoke are a powerful influence on their children. They think they can get away with the attitude of "Do as I say, not as I do", but their lectures on the dangers of smoking are wasted if their children see them puffing away.

As a parent you might think your children will listen to the wisdom of one who knows from experience, yet all the child sees is a grown-up smoking apparently out of choice, so of course they conclude that it must be giving them some wonderful pleasure or crutch.

The myth of pleasure or a crutch is promoted by everyone who smokes. After all, everyone knows smoking is a killer that burns your money, makes you unfit and antisocial and turns you into a slave, so what other possible reason could smokers have for continuing to do it?

ALL SMOKERS LIE

The trouble is, smokers convince themselves with the same Big Con. They have to because they can't live with the truth. They lie to others and they lie to themselves because the alternative is too unbearable.

It's bad enough being a smoker when you block your mind to the filth, the poison, the wheezing and coughing, the slavery and humiliation; if you had to face up to the grim reality day after day, life would not seem worth living.

So it suits smokers to buy into the myth because then they can pretend that there is a good reason for smoking and that they're not as helpless as it seems. Tragically, they begin to believe their own lies, as well as those of other smokers.

There are few things more pathetic than a smoker's lies. I was the worst! They lie that they haven't smoked when they reek of smoke. They lie about how much they smoke. They lie that they can take it or leave it. They lie that they will quit.

All these lies are really an attempt to convince nobody but themselves. It is the only alternative to admitting they are pathetic, helpless slaves who get no pleasure or crutch from smoking and can't understand why they can't just quit.

LURING YOU BACK IN

You will find it useful to recognize the influence of other smokers and to harness this knowledge to help you in your own escape. All too often smokers try to scupper the efforts of those who are attempting to quit. The thought of someone escaping the prison camp unnerves them because if that person succeeds, it challenges their own belief that escape is impossible and, therefore, not worth trying. As long as you have the fear of success, another smoker's escape will unsettle you. You feel like the last person left on the sinking ship.

Even when you do succeed in escaping, you will find there are always smokers ready to try and lure you back into the trap.

Make sure you are not vulnerable by preparing yourself in advance for the typical scenarios when a smoker's lies might snare you.

These scenarios are very often linked to a crisis: a car crash, a bereavement, a job loss, the break-up of a relationship... when these things happen there always seems to be a smoker on hand, ready to "comfort" you with a cigarette.

These smokers aren't evil. They genuinely want to help. It's just that they don't regard you as a non-smoker; they see you as a smoker who just happens not to be smoking at the moment. Because of the brainwashing, they assume that, like all smokers, the thing you really want at this difficult time is a cigarette.

Just as smokers get youngsters hooked by offering them freebies, they do the same to adults who succumb to the temptation.

Your smoking friend is there with the supply but warns you, "You'll get hooked again."

"No way!" you insist. "I just need one now. I'd never buy them."

But by smoking the one you've started the cycle of addiction and soon you're back asking for another. The smoker is secretly pleased that you're back for more – it makes them feel less stupid about their own addiction.

But their generosity only extends so far and soon you feel the pressure to repay the cigarettes they've given you. The dreadful moment comes when you find yourself buying a packet and suffering the humiliation of feeling like a failure.

Only a few days earlier you were a non-smoker who swore you would never buy cigarettes again. Now you're having to explain to your family and friends why you couldn't last.

To begin with you protest that you only bought them to repay your smoking friend but you know the truth. You're back in the trap.

THE MIRACLE OF UNCLE JOHN

When you believe that smoking provides some sort of pleasure or crutch, it's not surprising that you might feel you're helping a friend in need when you offer them a cigarette in a crisis. The delusion is powerful and convincing until you are shown the truth. But some of the lies that smokers tell in order to justify their decision to smoke are so far-fetched it's absurd.

A classic example is the myth of Uncle John. Uncle John is a character who crops up regularly in debates about smoking. He's a smoker who claims to have smoked 40 a day since the age of 14 and enjoyed every single one of them. Now here he is, in his 80s and still going strong. In fact, he claims never to have had a day's sickness in his life!

The implication is not just that smoking doesn't harm you, but that it's actually good for you!

People who argue in favour of smoking love to wheel out Uncle John as their star witness – living proof that all the health risks linked to smoking are not to be believed. Smokers cling doggedly to Uncle John to counteract the terrifying statistics society insists on throwing at us.

On the evidence of one example, they are trying to build an argument against the irrefutable evidence of seven million people who die as a result of smoking each year.

Then they bring out Auntie Jane, poor dear, who never smoked a cigarette in her life yet died from lung cancer at the age of 50.

THE RIGHT TO SMOKE

On top of this, there is the human rights argument: "Everybody should be free to choose whether or not they take the risk of smoking."

This is the stance of movements like "Forest", which labels itself the "voice and friend of the smoker". Forest members use a variety of spurious arguments to try to justify their collective slavery to nicotine addiction. For example, they state that tobacco sales bring in billions in taxation. So never mind the people who lose their lives as a result, it's all justified by the money!

They also argue that the public smoking ban has led to many older smokers no longer going to bars but drinking and smoking at home instead – the implication being that old people are being forced into social isolation by the ban on smoking in public places. It's not the smoking ban that's forcing them into isolation; it's their addiction to nicotine, an addiction that Forest works hard to maintain.

Forest epitomizes the false belief that smokers are in control of their smoking and their decision to smoke is a rational choice. They are missing two vital points:

1. Smokers have no freedom anyway. They do not choose to get hooked any more than a fly chooses to get trapped by the pitcher plant. Neither do they choose to remain smokers.

2. Smokers do not enjoy smoking or vaping. They only think they do because they're drug addicts, and so they feel most miserable when they're not allowed to smoke.

Forest's support for the freedom of the individual does not extend to legalizing heroin. Neither does it protect the rights of non-smokers to breathe clean air. Forest is funded by the tobacco industry, as is the UK Vaping Industry Association (UKVIA). Why do you think they do that?!!

〰〰〰〰〰〰〰〰〰〰〰〰〰〰〰〰〰〰〰〰〰〰〰〰〰〰〰〰〰〰

Exercise: **YOUR FREEDOM OF CHOICE**

While you're thinking about the right to choose, ask yourself these questions:

1. How many non-smokers would you say there are in the world who wish they were smokers?

2. How many ex-smokers do you think there are in the world who wish they were still smokers?

3. How many smokers do you know who, if they could now go back to the time when they lit that first cigarette, would still choose to light it?

If you've been completely honest, your answers will be:

1. None

2. None

3. None

〰〰〰〰〰〰〰〰〰〰〰〰〰〰〰〰〰〰〰〰〰〰〰〰〰〰〰〰〰〰

Forest and UKVIA are typical of the wilful smokers and vapers who like to fly in the face of popular opinion. They believe the myth that smoking gives them some kind of pleasure or crutch but, like everyone in the prison camp, the real motivation behind their continued smoking is

FEAR

Fear that they won't be able to enjoy or cope with life without smoking

Fear that they've got to go through some terrible ordeal to quit

Fear that they can never be completely free from the craving

It doesn't dawn on them that non-smokers never suffer any of these fears, or that the cigarette, or e-cigarette, far from relieving their fears, causes them. The fear of success is an illusion created by a myth. Yet the fears are so great that they override the very real dangers created by smoking and vaping. If you vape, make no mistake, the tobacco industry's involvement in vaping means only one thing: you're the victim.

ROLE MODELS

The influence of smokers on one another is reminiscent of George Orwell's *1984*. The creation of a society in which the people control each other through false information and fear sounds like a work of fiction, but it's something we have witnessed in real life through history and it is exactly how smokers influence one another today.

In *1984*, Big Brother, the embodiment of the system, appears to the public on "telescreens". Orwell was ahead of his time in recognizing the influence of movies and television. Hollywood and TV have played a major role in perpetuating the illusion that smoking is glamorous, cool, intellectual, interesting. The movie industry has become incredibly sophisticated in finding new ways to awe our senses but the one sense that remains detached from the action on the screen is the sense of smell.

Consequently, directors are able to portray smoking in a glamorous light, without having to deal with the reality that kissing, or even being in a room with someone who smokes is a foul experience, no matter how good-looking, sexy, eloquent, or cool they appear to be.

On-screen heroes help to perpetuate the myths about smoking. I've already talked about the image of Sherlock Holmes smoking his pipe as he tries to think his way through the latest mysterious case. The portrayal of smoking as an aid to concentration is commonplace in movies, as is the portrayal as a social crutch, a relief for stress, a relaxation aid, a natural accompaniment for a drink, a meal and sex.

Smoking film stars are just more prisoners in the camp but their influence is particularly strong. The power of the big screen is extraordinary. From Greta Garbo to Leonardo DiCaprio, the image of the movie star with a cigarette has encouraged countless people to start smoking. During the 1970s, Hollywood woke up to the dangers of smoking and made its own attempt to cut down, with smoking appearing far less in films than it did in the days of Humphrey Bogart, James Dean and Audrey Hepburn, but today Tinseltown appears to be well and truly hooked again. In truth, it never really broke free. Whether it was Sylvester Stallone, Faye Dunaway, Steve McQueen, Clint Eastwood, John Travolta, Olivia Newton John, Arnold Schwarzenegger, Bruce Willis, Al Pacino, Sharon Stone, Meg Ryan, Julia Roberts, Sigourney Weaver, Leonardo DiCaprio, Brad Pitt, Hugh Jackman, Uma Thurman, Scarlett Johansson, Cate Blanchett, or Ryan Reynolds, they've all conspired, to a greater or lesser extent, to make cigarettes and smoking appear cool, sexy, or sophisticated. Do you really think that any of them would have appeared any less desirable or cool, in any way, if they hadn't smoked? Or less tough? Or less sophisticated? Look at the names. Remember the movies.

This isn't, by any means, an exhaustive list at all. As you read it, I have no doubt that you will be able to recall many more smoking moments in the movies that you've loved throughout your life. The list spans more than 70 years.

No doubt by the time you're reading this the latest Hollywood star will have added themselves to the list. Over the years, many Hollywood stars have played a leading role in luring people into the nicotine trap and they have been paid handsomely to do so. It's not just movie stars either. TV celebrities, models, pop stars and even criminals can be powerful role models, and if they smoke, their fans will smoke.

SEEING THE TRUTH TOO LATE

There are two things that make smokers stop lying: one is escaping the trap and becoming a happy non-smoker; the other is the realization that you have not escaped the deadly consequences of smoking.

Hollywood legend Yul Brynner had the courage to admit that he had been stupid after he knew that his smoking was bringing his life to a premature end. "Marlboro Man" Wayne McLaren became an active anti-smoking campaigner when he was diagnosed with terminal cancer. Tragically, he was one of five actors who have appeared as the cowboy on Marlboro adverts to have died of smoking-related diseases.

Movie writer and director Joe Eszterhas developed throat cancer as a result of heavy smoking, after which he expressed deep regret for the way he promoted smoking in his movie *Basic Instinct*, so influential that it led to a tobacco company launching a brand of "Basic" cigarettes. Writing in the *New York Times*, Eszterhas said:

"Remembering all this, I find it hard to forgive myself. I have been an accomplice to the murders of untold numbers of human beings. I am admitting this only because I have made a deal with God. Spare me, I said, and I will try to stop others from committing the same crimes I did.

"Eighteen months ago, I was diagnosed with throat cancer, the result of a lifetime of smoking. I am alive but maimed. Much of my larynx is gone. I have some difficulty speaking; others have some difficulty understanding me."

Too late in the day, the likes of Eszterhas, Brynner and McLaren realized the folly of smoking and tried to make amends by using their influence to discourage others from smoking. If only they had used their influence in this way from the start.

When you're faced with the reality of a terminal disease, it's impossible to keep fooling yourself with the Big Con. Smokers who quit when it's too late still display the characteristics of elation at finally breaking free from the slavery of nicotine addiction, even amid the sadness of their premature demise. Their determination to stop others from making the same mistake is completely heartfelt. Sadly, they are not left with enough time to undo the damage they did through their influence as smokers.

As we see movie stars and other role models, who we once regarded as demi-gods, dying miserably as the result of smoking, it dawns on us that they weren't smoking because it's cool and glamorous but because they were conned, just like we were, and they wish they hadn't become smokers, just as we do. You don't want to wait until you're faced with the reality of a premature death before you convince yourself that there is absolutely no benefit whatsoever to smoking. You have so much to live for. It's time for you to stop being part of the Big Con.

Anyone can walk free from the prison camp – all you have to do is ignore the influence of other smokers, see through the myth and make your own rational decision to stop smoking.

SUBSTITUTES DON'T WORK

AS YOU PREPARE TO SMOKE YOUR FINAL CIGARETTE OR E-CIGARETTE TOMORROW, IT'S TIME TO DECIDE WHAT IT IS YOU REALLY WANT. ARE YOU LOOKING FOR A WAY TO KEEP TAKING NICOTINE WITHOUT THE LIFE-THREATENING SIDE-EFFECTS OR ARE YOU LOOKING TO BE FREE FROM NICOTINE ADDICTION ALTOGETHER?

THE BIG TOBACCO PROBLEM

No one other than those with vested interests disputes that smoking is a major problem. Even the tobacco companies have been forced to admit to the terrible health risks associated with their product and carry graphic warnings on their packets, leaving smokers in no doubt about what they're letting themselves in for. The fact that these revolting images fail to dissuade people from buying cigarettes proves that trying to convince smokers to quit by frightening them simply doesn't work.

Over the years, the tobacco companies have invested heavily in trying to develop alternatives to cigarettes. It's easy to understand why. The industry makes staggering amounts of money from peddling a product that everybody is terrified of; imagine what it could make for a product that had the same irresistible qualities but didn't disable its customers quite so quickly. Current smokers would pay even more than they spend now on cigarettes, and all those non-smokers who avoided becoming addicts because of the health risks would rush to join them.

Big Tobacco began by trying to introduce a nicotine-free cigarette. It flopped. If you've ever tried herbal cigarettes, you'll know why. Herbal cigarettes are foul, smelly things that give no illusion of satisfaction at all. Your favourite brand of cigarettes smelled and tasted foul too when you first started smoking, but you persevered. Nobody persevered with herbal cigarettes. It quickly became apparent that you could smoke these things for the rest of your life without ever believing that you were enjoying them. Why? Because they contained no nicotine.

Big Tobacco learnt from its experiment that nicotine addiction isn't just a hazard of smoking, it is the ONLY REASON people continue to smoke. The fact that they, and Big Pharma, have used this experience to justify the use of e-cigarettes as an "aid to quitting" is telling. By providing "0% nicotine" vape liquid they maintain the myth that the idea is for the smoker to switch to vaping, then gradually move towards so-called "vape juice" that has zero nicotine content. The fact is, very few, if any, vapers ever actually achieve that. If you're a vaper, do you know anyone that has? They remain hooked on nicotine and continue to consume nicotine in ever-increasing (rather than decreasing) doses. That's the way drug addiction always works.

Doctors faced with patients who were smoking themselves to death started to prescribe nicotine alternatives, such as nicotine gum and nicotine patches, in the hope that these products would satisfy their patients' drug addiction while sparing them the appalling effects of smoking.

The tobacco companies weren't so interested in patient health. They had spotted another opportunity. As governments began to get tough on smoking, banning it in public places, smokeless nicotine products enabled Big Tobacco and Big Pharma to keep peddling their drugs and keep their customers hooked.

Since then all sorts of new nicotine products have come to the market. There's snus from Scandinavia, a teabag-like pouch of ground tobacco that's placed in the mouth, passing the drug into the bloodstream through the gums. Snus is sold in flavours like cranberry, eucalyptus and peppermint, which give it the appearance of confectionery. It's anything but.

Snus is sold with the following warning: "This tobacco product damages your health and is addictive." Hardly a harmless alternative to smoking.

Another fairly recent development is dissolvable tobacco. R.J. Reynolds makes a range of Camel-branded dissolvable tobacco products, including Orbs, Sticks and Strips. There are also Marlboro-branded Sticks. All these products are tobacco in an alternative form, sweetened, flavoured and designed to dissolve in the mouth. Like snus, they are an evolution of the cruder chewing tobacco popular among cowboys in the Wild West (and baseball players), the difference being that you don't have to spit. The flavouring makes your tobacco-infused saliva more palatable. But the principle is the same: nicotine passes into your bloodstream through the thin membrane of the gums.

These products may not deliver the toxic fumes of smoking, but they do deliver a bigger dose of the drug. Camel dissolvables deliver up to 3.1mg, nicotine gum up to 4mg. Smokers typically inhale 1mg per cigarette. So whether you're getting your substitutes from Big Tobacco or the doctor, the effect is the same:

BOTH INCREASE YOUR NICOTINE ADDICTION

The pharmaceutical industry and the tobacco industry are both involved in the production, marketing and sale of e-cigarettes. That fact alone should make you aware that you face a big choice: stay trapped inside the nicotine prison and keep filling the bulging pockets of the nicotine industry (and pay a fortune by way of the sales taxes on the products), or simply set yourself free. As an example, UK tax revenues from tobacco sales are over £12bn ($16.4bn) a year. The health costs of treating smokers are around £3bn ($4.1bn). No wonder the UK government has made it so easy for vaping companies to sell their wares… they're desperate to keep making money from the addiction. They want you, and your kids, to remain lifelong addicts.

NO ILLUSIONS

Smokers make up all sorts of spurious reasons why they smoke. They think it looks cool, sophisticated, glamorous. They think it's sociable. They like the ritual. All these illusions go out of the window when you're taking your nicotine in pellets or via a weird-looking "vape tank".

A nicotine junkie getting their fix is no different from a heroin addict sticking a needle in their arm. Do you think heroin addicts enjoy giving themselves injections? Most people hate needles. Some faint at the sight of them. But heroin addicts can't wait for the needle to find a vein. Is that because they're anticipating a tremendous high? Or is it because they know that the panic and misery they're suffering is about to be relieved? The fact is, they no longer know the difference.

Watch the reaction of a heroin addict as the drug enters their bloodstream. It's not pleasure; it's relief, like the relief of taking off tight shoes. It's not the beginning of something good; it's the ending of something bad – albeit for just a short time. It's the thief giving his victim

$10 back from the $100 he stole, and the victim being fooled into gratitude.

Heroin addicts don't enjoy the needle going into their arm. That's just the way they get their drug. Without going into graphic detail, the process of finding a vein anywhere in their body becomes a truly humiliating, shameful and degrading process for the addict. There are clear similarities between all drug addictions. However, there is one key difference: heroin addicts know they only inject themselves to get the heroin, whereas nicotine addicts believe they smoke because they enjoy smoking for its own sake. The same goes for vaping.

The way smoking traps the smoker is much more subtle than the way heroin traps the heroin addict. Smokers think they enjoy smoking because it appears to relieve the empty, insecure feeling that they perceive to be part of normal life. Non-smokers don't suffer it and neither did you before you started smoking. But because of the gradual decline that I described on Day Two, smokers regard the empty, insecure feeling of nicotine withdrawal as "normal", and as they slide further into the trap, they continually adjust their perception of "normal", not realizing that they're slipping way below a genuinely normal, healthy level of wellbeing.

When you quit, you will be amazed how far below a genuine level of normality smoking or vaping dragged you down. Without the panic of nicotine addiction, you will feel more relaxed, confident, happy and healthy ALL THE TIME.

A couple of centuries ago, nicotine addicts got their fix by sniffing dust up their nose in the form of snuff. In the Wild West and on the baseball pitch, they stuck a plug of tobacco between their cheek and gum and continually spat out the repulsive juice. If you've ever tried chewing tobacco and made the mistake of swallowing, you'll understand the need to keep spitting. The taste is pure poison.

Be under no illusions, whether you sniff snuff, chew tobacco, smoke cigarettes, use snus, suck nicotine sticks, chew nicotine gum, stick a patch on your skin, or vape, the methods of taking nicotine have nothing to do with pleasure. It's all about getting the drug into your bloodstream and keeping you hooked.

INCREASING THE DOSE

I've talked about the fact that cigarette substitutes deliver a higher dose of nicotine than cigarettes. In addition to that, most smokers who use e-cigarettes in an attempt to quit will continue to smoke as well. They smoke when they can and vape when they can't. The end result? They take in even more nicotine than they did before. The addiction isn't getting weaker and the nicotine industry makes money at both ends.

It hardly takes a genius to realize that giving a drug addict the drug they're addicted to in bigger doses can't possibly help them to break their addiction. Yet governments and the medical community, egged on by the pharmaceutical companies that manufacture NRT, have ploughed millions into developing more and more such products, which line the pockets of the super-rich drugs companies and keep nicotine addicts trapped in the prison camp. It's a scandal. Much of the money is public funding, paid for by taxpayers.

In fact, in the UK the major cancer research organization and the public health authority have promoted the use of e-cigarettes in expensive advertising campaigns. Now, Cancer Research UK is an amazing charity, but I think the kind people who donate would be extremely surprised to see them funding adverts for e-cigarettes that will fill the already bulging bank accounts of the tobacco industry and the pharmaceutical industry, don't you? The clue is in the charity's name "Cancer Research UK". It really is as if the world has gone entirely mad.

Meanwhile, more and more nicotine products are finding their way to market that don't even pretend to help you quit but are marketed as a permanent alternative to cigarettes. Do you really want a permanent alternative to cigarettes? Or would you rather be free of addiction?

POISONED BY YOUR DOCTOR

It's utterly irresponsible for a doctor to prescribe nicotine products to a smoker who wants help to quit. You're being prescribed a powerful poison for a condition that only exists because you're already taking that poison, a condition for which the only cure is to STOP taking the poison.

Writer, broadcaster and professional poker player Victoria Coren Mitchell described the medical profession's eagerness to have UK smokers switch to vaping (with taxpayer-funded e-cigarettes) as follows:

"That the state would seriously consider decanting money from our beautiful, beleaguered National Health Service into the coffers of British American Tobacco, while ignoring Allen Carr's breakthrough ever since publication [of his quit smoking method in 1985], is as though Alexander Fleming had discovered penicillin in 1985 and the Health Service, having told nobody about it for 33 years, was buying Louis Vuitton scarves in bulk for throat infections.

"Except, for that comparison to work properly, they'd need to be Louis Vuitton scarves that might cause emphysema themselves if you wore them long enough."

The dictionary definition of nicotine describes it as "A poisonous, addictive, colourless, oily liquid which is the chief constituent of tobacco and insecticides." The *A–Z of Medicinal Drugs* lists the side-effects: "Nausea, dizziness, headache, influenza-like symptoms, palpitations, indigestion, insomnia and vivid dreams, and muscle aches. Skin patches may cause local reactions. Sprays can cause throat and nasal irritation, nose bleeds, watery eyes and sensations in the ear. Gums can irritate the throat and cause mouth ulcers and sometimes swelling of the tongue. Inhalators can cause a sore mouth or throat, mouth ulcers, a swollen tongue, cough, running nose, and sinusitis."

More evidence informing the long-term harmful effects of vaping is coming to light each month, but of course those with vested interests deny their validity. Does that sound familiar? It should do. It's direct from the playbook of 1950s Big Tobacco.

WHY WE EVEN CONSIDER SUBSTITUTES

"Whatever vaping may or may not do to smokers, at least it spares them the carcinogenic fumes of smoking." That's one of the main arguments put forward by the medical profession when promoting nicotine products which aren't burned. And if you're happy to remain a nicotine addict for the rest of your life, they might have a point. But isn't your reason for reading this book to get free from being controlled by nicotine? It will be decades before the true extent of vaping's harmful effects are known. Deep down inside, you know though, don't you? You're not a fool. You instinctively know that vaping isn't the solution. Otherwise, you simply wouldn't be reading this book.

As long as you remain hooked on nicotine, you will always be vulnerable to becoming a smoker again. Remember, the only reason anyone smokes is to get the nicotine. So if you're craving nicotine and you're offered a cigarette, do you think you'll be able to resist the temptation?

With Easyway, you don't have to resist the temptation.

We remove the temptation altogether by helping you to escape the slavery to nicotine.

The other medical argument is that vaping or other nicotine products help to ease smokers off their addiction by giving you something to keep you topped up with nicotine while you deal with whatever it is that you think keeps you wanting to smoke. Then, when you think you've kicked the habit, you gradually reduce the nicotine dose until you're off it completely and you don't miss it any more.

But of course, it's not that simple. If it was, nicotine patches and gum would have been a resounding success, e-cigarettes would be rare as their users successfully weaned themselves off the addiction and the world would be cured of smoking. Clearly, it's been an abject failure.

Vaping doesn't work as a cure for smoking because it is based on three false beliefs:

1. That the physical withdrawal is painful.

2. That smoking is a habit.

3. That people don't mind being addicted.

THE PHYSICAL WITHDRAWAL IS ALMOST IMPERCEPTIBLE;
SMOKING IS NOT A HABIT - IT'S DRUG ADDICTION;
NO ONE WANTS TO BE ADDICTED TO ANYTHING

The fabulous thing about understanding the addiction is that, although highly effective in hooking its victims, the addiction itself is actually extremely weak and easy to break free from... as long as you know how.

For anyone who still believes that smoking or vaping gives them some sort of benefit or crutch, cutting down gradually is a real struggle. It goes against everything their mind and body are crying out for. As you learned yesterday, the nicotine trap takes you on a downward spiral because each cigarette never fully satisfies the craving created by the one before, so you are always wanting to increase the dose.

THE TENDENCY WITH ALL DRUGS IS TO TAKE MORE, NOT LESS

DECISION TIME

So it's time to decide what you really want. All smokers dream of a substitute that gives you that feeling of relaxation you get when you light up, without any of the disadvantages – the failing health, the cost, slavery, filth and stigma.

GOOD NEWS!

This is exactly what you get when you quit smoking or vaping and get free from nicotine.

That feeling of relaxation is what non-smokers have all the time. It is the feeling of relief from nicotine craving. Non-smokers don't suffer from nicotine craving. The only reason you smoke or vape is to feel like a non-smoker or non-vaper feels ALL THE TIME.

In order to become a happy non-smoker or non-vaper, you do need to conquer two enemies, but habit has nothing to do with it and you won't suffer any pain. One of those enemies is the Little Monster in your body, which feeds on nicotine and cries out when it's hungry. The cries of the Little Monster are so slight as to be almost imperceptible. You don't need a gradual weaning process to cope with the physical sensation of withdrawal.

The only threat from the Little Monster is that it wakes up the Big Monster in your brain, which interprets the Little Monster's cries as "I want a cigarette".

The Big Monster makes you fixate on having a cigarette and causes you to feel deprived and miserable if you can't. Continue to feed the Little Monster and you prolong the life of both your enemies.

NON-NICOTINE SUBSTITUTES

Anything that you use as a substitute for smoking perpetuates the illusion that you're making a sacrifice when you quit.

Sweets, chocolate and normal chewing gum are common substitutes used by smokers trying to quit. Whenever they feel the nicotine craving, they have a sweet, chocolate or gum instead of smoking. This is only moving the problem, not solving it. The empty, insecure feeling of the body withdrawing from nicotine feels the same as hunger, but food does not relieve it. It might take your mind off the craving for a little while, but it doesn't remove the feeling of sacrifice. As long as the Big Monster is still alive in your brain, you will never be free from the desire to smoke.

WORRIED ABOUT YOUR WEIGHT?

YOU MAY BE AWARE OF THE THEORY THAT SMOKING HELPS TO KEEP YOUR WEIGHT DOWN, AND WORRYING THAT YOU WILL GAIN WEIGHT IF YOU QUIT. AS I'VE MENTIONED PREVIOUSLY, THERE IS NO NEED TO WORRY AT ALL. THE EFFECT OF SMOKING ON WEIGHT IS A MYTH. EASYWAY WILL SHOW YOU HOW TO QUIT WITHOUT PUTTING ON ANY WEIGHT AT ALL. I WANT TO TAKE A FEW MOMENTS TO RECAP AND ELABORATE ON THIS IMPORTANT ISSUE FURTHER.

CONFLICTING EVIDENCE

The myth that smoking keeps you thin is based on the evidence of people who try to quit with the willpower method and find themselves putting on weight. Naturally, they assume that the cigarettes were keeping them thin. There are plenty of people like this about and remember, smokers who quit with the willpower method love to let everyone know all about their struggle.

We hear a lot less from those who quit without any problem. There are enough examples of people who lose weight after quitting to cast considerable doubt on any theory that smoking keeps you thin. There are also plenty of overweight smokers who'll be scratching their head at this theory.

I used to joke, "I'm not overweight, I'm just six inches shorter than I should be." During my years as a heavy smoker, I was a heavy man too, a constant two stone overweight, even though I ate only one meal a day!

Smoking did not make me thin, yet whenever I tried to quit I somehow gained more weight... with one notable exception. When I stopped smoking for good, I lost two stone within six months of smoking my final cigarette.

So what are we supposed to believe? Does smoking make you put on weight or does it keep your weight down? Let's unravel the myth and see the true picture.

HUNGER VS NICOTINE WITHDRAWAL

At the end of the last chapter I mentioned that the empty, insecure feeling of nicotine withdrawing from the body feels the same as hunger. It's a feeling that's so slight that it rarely captures your attention but it does trigger automatic responses. With hunger, your body is asking you to respond by feeding it with food; with nicotine withdrawal, the Little Monster is demanding you feed it with nicotine.

The feelings are the same, their sources are very different. One is a natural survival instinct, the other is drug addiction. And most importantly, you can't satisfy the cravings by substituting nicotine for food or vice versa.

SMOKING WILL NOT SATISFY HUNGER

FOOD WILL NOT STOP THE NICOTINE CRAVINGS

If your car is overheating, it could be because the engine is low on oil or because the cooling system is low on water. If you top up the oil with water or top up the coolant with oil, you won't fix the problem. In fact, you'll destroy the machine!

People who try to quit with the willpower method try to satisfy the craving, or take their mind off it, by treating it as if it was hunger. They substitute cigarettes with junk food. Chewing gum and sweets are the common choice. Of course, they don't even satisfy hunger, let alone nicotine craving. So you move on to more substantial foods in your efforts to satisfy what feels like a permanent hunger.

The willpower method perpetuates the myth that you're making a sacrifice, so when you quit with willpower your body and brain are always expecting little rewards. If you regard cakes, biscuits and chocolate bars as rewards, or burgers, chips and other junk foods, you will eat to excess to overcome the feeling of deprivation.

This is why people who quit with the willpower method put on weight. But because of the myth that smoking keeps your weight down, you assume the weight gain is due to "giving up" cigarettes.

When you quit with Easyway, you don't feel like you're "giving up" anything; only making wonderful gains. There's no psychological need for extra rewards.

WHY SOME SMOKERS LOSE WEIGHT

The confusion between hunger and nicotine craving also explains why some smokers do get thinner. Instead of eating when hungry, they smoke. First thing in the morning, when you wake up, both smokers and non-smokers instinctively relieve a number of needs. We relieve our bladders, we relieve our thirst and non-smokers also relieve their hunger. Smokers, however, are more likely to light a cigarette.

As the hunger intensifies, the smoker continues to confuse the need with their craving for nicotine, so they smoke more. Most smokers, however, have the opposite problem. They eat when they feel the craving for nicotine. Of course, eating doesn't satisfy the Little Monster. Neither does smoking – not fully. Because of your tolerance to the poison, you go through life with what feels like a permanent hunger. The tendency is to try and satisfy this feeling by eating as well as smoking.

When opportunities to smoke are restricted – as they are increasingly these days – smokers will eat instead. This isn't a conscious choice; they are instinctively responding to a sensation that feels just like hunger. If they could smoke they would, but without being able to smoke they reach for the next available option.

If smoking actually helped you to keep your weight down, you would expect most heavy smokers to be slim. In fact, most heavy smokers are overweight.

WHAT IS HUNGER?

Hunger is a crucial and ingenious part of your body's survival toolkit, which we talked about on Day One. It works rather like the fuel gauge on your car. When your body is running low on the vital nutrients it needs, it sends a signal to your brain that feels like an emptiness in your stomach, and your brain responds by looking for things to eat.

When your car's fuel gauge approaches empty, what do you do? Drive to the nearest lake or river and fill up with water? Drive to a builder's yard and fill up with sand? Of course not, you pull in at the next petrol station and fill up with the right type of fuel.

Your body is just as specific about the fuel it needs. When it signals hunger, it's not asking for any old rubbish to be forced into your digestive system; it's asking for specific vitamins, minerals, fibre, protein, carbohydrate, etc., which your body needs to stay healthy and strong. Respond to hunger by filling up with junk food and you won't satisfy that need; therefore, you will not satisfy your hunger, and so you will keep eating and put on weight.

You can read more about hunger and how to be your ideal weight without dieting or feeling deprived in *Allen Carr's Lose Weight Now* or *Allen Carr's Good Sugar, Bad Sugar*.

BLINDED BY SCIENCE

Like most of the smoking myths, the one about smoking keeping you thin is reinforced by certain "so-called" experts, who have added a couple of scientific twists to the theory. One is that smoking speeds up your metabolism, which means you burn off fat faster.

If this was the case, how do they explain why most heavy smokers are overweight and why smokers who quit with Easyway tend to lose weight after they stop smoking? Surely if their metabolism slowed down they would put on weight.

Another theory is that smoking is an appetite suppressant. In other words, it reduces your desire for food. This theory is based on three facts:

1. Many smokers who quit eat more and put on weight. This is because when smokers quit with the willpower method they

feel deprived and try to substitute cigarettes by eating and drinking more.

2. Smoking reduces the pangs. This is the only reason anyone smokes – to relieve the pangs of withdrawal from nicotine. But smoking only relieves nicotine withdrawal, and only partially. The confusion between nicotine craving and hunger fools smokers into thinking they're hungry when they're craving nicotine and if they smoke in that moment, the partial relief of the nicotine craving in that moment fools them into thinking the cigarette has relieved their hunger.

3. Hunger pangs come and go. Non-smokers know that they don't have to eat every time they feel a hunger pang. It's a very mild sensation and it will subside after a short time if they ignore it. However, if a smoker feels a hunger pang and lights up, they credit the cigarette when the pang subsides. In fact, the pang would have subsided anyway. They have no idea this is what happens to non-smokers.

You can always find a "so-called" expert coming up with complicated theories when the truth is staring us all in the face.

YOU WILL PUT ON WEIGHT WHEN YOU STOP SMOKING IF YOU START SUBSTITUTING FOOD FOR NICOTINE

But when you use Allen Carr's Easyway, that doesn't happen. When you quit, the Little Monster will continue to cry out for its fix for a few days. The feeling is so slight as to be almost imperceptible but if you think you're making a sacrifice it will make you feel deprived and miserable. With this method you smoke your final cigarette knowing that you're not sacrificing anything. On the contrary, you're making marvellous gains. So you can rejoice in the death throes of the Little Monster without feeling any need for substitutes. Find that hard to believe? Just you wait and see.

ACHIEVING YOUR IDEAL WEIGHT

There are two factors that determine whether you lose or gain weight. One is diet; the other is exercise. If you take in more fuel than you burn off, you will gain weight. Burn off more than you take in and you will lose weight.

There are factors that influence the amount you consume and the amount you burn, and smoking is one of them. The confusion between hunger and nicotine craving makes some smokers eat more and others eat less. The health impact of smoking makes all smokers less fit to take exercise.

One of the marvellous gains you can look forward to is feeling more energetic and healthy. Smokers tend to shy away from physical exercise because they find even the simplest of tasks can leave them out of breath. The self-consciousness and lack of confidence also deter them from the exercise environment. They retreat into the security of the prison and try to comfort themselves by smoking more. This is another reason why most smokers are overweight.

A key instruction with Easyway is not to alter your lifestyle just because you stop smoking. I will explain why later. But when you quit, you may well feel more inclined to take regular exercise because you've got the energy and confidence for it. Exercise gets the adrenalin

flowing and makes you feel great. It's the best stimulant there is –
a genuine high!

If you're out of condition, start slowly and don't push yourself too
hard. There's no need. You've got the rest of your life.

Once you've solved your smoking problem, you'll have so much
more confidence and energy that you'll be far better equipped to solve
other problems, such as weight.

If you've been relying on smoking to keep your weight down, you
can abandon that policy now. Any success you've had in keeping your
weight down is in spite of smoking, not because of it. Believe that
smoking gives you any kind of benefit and you're more likely to put
on weight, either by remaining a smoker and feeling confused or by
quitting and feeling deprived and substituting (eating and drinking
instead of smoking).

THE FINAL PROOF

If you're still not convinced that the "so-called" experts have got
it wrong, ask yourself this: Why is there no such thing as The Diet
Cigarette? Imagine if Big Tobacco had conclusive proof that cigarettes
kept your weight down; don't you think they would shout about it
from the rooftops and bring out a brand specifically aimed at dieters?
So why haven't they? Quite simply because

SMOKING DOES NOT HELP YOU LOSE WEIGHT

If it did, the manufacturers would say so. No one could stop them.
Instead they use celebrity promotions and product placement to
imply it! It's phoney! Don't swallow their lies any more.

ALL SMOKERS ARE THE SAME

THE ADDICTIVE PERSONALITY MYTH FEEDS THE BELIEF THAT SOME SMOKERS ARE MORE SUSCEPTIBLE TO THE NICOTINE TRAP THAN OTHERS AND SOME CAN CONTROL THEIR SMOKING BETTER THAN OTHERS. SO LET'S TRY TO IDENTIFY WHICH TYPE OF SMOKER YOU ARE AND WHICH YOU WOULD LIKE TO BE.

WOMEN SMOKERS

Tobacco companies don't claim that cigarettes keep you slim because they can't – it's not true. Advertising, for all its vices, still has to carry at least a modicum of truth. All they can do is perpetuate the myth by putting their products in the hands of slender movie stars, models and other female icons. Sadly, the marketing works.

Not so long ago, women smokers were very much in the minority. Now, in many countries, they outnumber men.

You could put this down to a shift in the social structure, which has seen women embrace many of the behaviours of men. The idea of gender roles is fast becoming outmoded, and so perhaps you consider it quite natural that women should smoke just as much as men. But that would suggest that, in the past, society was full of male smokers with wives and girlfriends who wished they could smoke too. In truth, those male smokers often did their smoking in secret because their wives and girlfriends were constantly pleading with them to stop. They could see it was a filthy, disgusting thing to do and that it was swallowing the household budget and threatening to leave them a widow. Quite simply, women didn't smoke because they had too much sense!

So why, now that fewer men are smoking, have we seen such soaring smoking statistics among women? Quite simply, the tobacco industry has made a concerted effort to hook women. Back in the 1970s, the proportion of men who smoked was roughly double the proportion of women. To an industry like Big Tobacco, a whole section of society that rejects its product like that is a whole potential new market. And so Big Tobacco began to make its products more feminine. Menthol flavouring, more elegant packets, slimmer cigarettes and rumours that smoking made you thin and helped to ease stress abounded.

Women were taking on more and more demanding lifestyles, combining full-time careers with motherhood and, in many cases, still being the ones who cooked dinner, made the children's lunches, ironed the shirts and cleaned the house. Brainwashed with the myth that smoking eases stress and keeps you slim, no wonder they reached for a cigarette whenever they found five minutes to themselves! So have women become more susceptible to the nicotine trap? Not at all. All that's happened is that Big Tobacco has gone after women with a vengeance, perpetuating the myths that lure us into the trap and keep us there, until we find the key to escape.

The key is seeing through the illusions and understanding the true picture: that smoking does not relieve stress, or provide any kind of crutch at all; neither does it suppress your appetite and help you stay slim. The truth is exactly what women used to tell their smoking husbands before they themselves were lured into the trap:

SMOKING DOES NOTHING FOR YOU WHATSOEVER

THE SACRIFICIAL MOTHER

I mentioned motherhood. This brings me to a major problem that is specific to women – smoking and pregnancy. It's long been known that smoking when pregnant harms the baby. Some women are lucky and find that, just as nature alters their eating habits to benefit both mother and unborn child, it also takes away their desire to smoke when pregnant. It's another example of the incredible machine constantly working to protect you.

Other women, however, are not so lucky. They make a conscious effort to stop but fail.

They spend the entire pregnancy feeling guilty and, even if the baby is born healthy, they can be left with a feeling of guilt for the rest of their lives. To allow young women to become hooked on nicotine and then make them feel guilty if they don't quit when pregnant is one of society's more shameful acts of hypocrisy. Even when an expectant mother does succeed in quitting, it's usually only for the duration of the pregnancy. Some light up the moment the cord is cut!

You can imagine why. The birth has gone well, mother and baby are fine, the anxiety is over, the pain and suffering momentarily forgotten and the mother's mood switches from exhaustion to the highest of highs: the two extremes that most strongly trigger the Big Monster to say, "I need a cigarette." Moreover, after all those months of resisting the temptation to smoke, and after going through the challenge of childbirth, the mother believes she deserves one – and who is going to tell her she's wrong!

Some new mothers resist the initial impulse but are caught out at a later date. Regrettably, very few women stop smoking permanently because of pregnancy. The blame doesn't lie with them. Addiction doesn't care if you're the expectant mother of a child.

A major problem for women smokers who stop during pregnancy is that they're not quitting for their own sake but for the sake of the baby. If you try to quit for the sake of someone else you will believe that you're making a sacrifice and will feel deprived. When you stop smoking it should be for the purely selfish reason that you're going to enjoy life a whole lot more as a non-smoker, you're not "giving up" anything and you will be happy to be free.

CUTTING DOWN

Many doctors, with the best of intentions, advise women to try to cut down on their smoking if they're finding it impossible to quit during pregnancy. The thinking is that a little of the poison will do less damage than a lot of it. This seems logical, but the truth is that it's actually harder to cut down than it is to quit smoking altogether.

Instead of being free from nicotine withdrawal after a few days, mother and baby are subjected to it for the whole nine months. Meanwhile, the illusion is ingrained in the mother's mind that she is making a sacrifice and each cigarette is incredibly precious. Once the baby is born, her motivation to go on depriving herself is gone and, like the dieter who reaches her target weight, she embarks on a binge to "reward" herself. Sadly, because of cutting down, many young mothers end up more hooked after giving birth than they were before the pregnancy. The lucky ones go off it as soon as they know they're pregnant.

There is a common belief among all smokers that people who smoke less are better off. This is a myth, as I will explain, but the fact that all smokers believe it proves that no smoker is happy that they smoke.

I have explained why the tendency with all addictions is to take more, not less. As your body builds a tolerance to the toxin, you require bigger doses of the drug to feel the same effect. It is only external restrictions, such as money and opportunity, that prevent all smokers from becoming heavy smokers.

Yet no one sets out to become a heavy smoker. We all assume we can control our intake, smoking only when we want to. What we don't realize, at least not when we first land in the trap, is that the addiction makes you want to smoke all the time. The slightly empty, insecure feeling of nicotine withdrawing from your body is what makes you smoke the next cigarette and, while that gives you the illusion of relief, it is not complete and it is only temporary.

The feeling returns soon after you put out your cigarette – the Little Monster starts crying for its next fix – and the Big Monster immediately starts nagging you to oblige.

Cutting down increases the value we place on each cigarette and decreases our desire to quit.

So anyone who restricts the amount they smoke is going against the compulsion of their addiction and will feel they are making a sacrifice. Heavy smokers smoke as much as they feel they want to, yet they envy other smokers who smoke less than them. Weird, isn't it?

〰〰〰〰〰〰〰〰〰〰〰〰〰〰〰〰〰〰〰〰〰〰〰〰〰〰〰〰〰〰

Exercise: **TWO QUESTIONS**

Think about this carefully. When it comes to deciding what type of smoker, vaper or nicotine addict you want to be, there are two questions you should ask yourself:

1. How much would you smoke or vape if you could choose your ideal amount?

Having decided how often you would like to smoke, the next question is:

2. Why don't you smoke, vape, imbibe that much now?

No one forces you to smoke, or vape, or snus, or chew tobacco. It is only you who takes the nicotine from the pack. If you want to do it less often, who's stopping you?

Smokers envy anyone who smokes less than them because they think they're getting the best of both worlds: they're getting their pleasure or crutch and they don't appear to be enslaved by smoking. In short, they appear to be in control of their smoking.

In fact, both beliefs are false. There is no pleasure or crutch from smoking and light smokers suffer just as much in the nicotine trap as heavy smokers. In fact, they suffer more because they are constantly fighting the urge to smoke more. The same goes for vapers.

Any smoker who has tried to cut down knows that restricting the amount you smoke through willpower will only work for a limited period at best.

When your smoking is restricted by factors such as smoking bans, it's easy to go without because there is no question of smoking. Just like the student in the exam, when you know that smoking is not an option, the Big Monster doesn't bother you. It's only when you can smoke but try to stop yourself from doing so that the Big Monster begins to torment you.

Some ex-smokers fall into the trap again because they grow overconfident and think they can have "just the one" without getting hooked. They still believe they have made a sacrifice, they think they deserve a reward and they think they can control their smoking. It's the same delusion that leads to smokers getting hooked in the first place. Even if you think you have many strong reasons for lighting up, you wouldn't light that one cigarette if you knew you would have to continue smoking for the rest of your life.

Be very clear about this:

THERE IS NO SUCH THING AS "JUST THE ONE"

If you smoke one cigarette, what's to stop you smoking the next and the next and the next? It doesn't matter how heavy a smoker you are,

THE NEXT CIGARETTE COULD BE THE ONE THAT KILLS YOU; THERE IS ALWAYS ANOTHER AND ANOTHER AND ANOTHER

A WORD TO THE WISE ABOUT "JOINTS"

Apologies to the many readers who have never/would never touch illicit drugs under any circumstances – you can feel free to skip this small section, especially if you find the subject distasteful. I make no apologies for covering it though, purely because it's an issue that arises for many, many smokers.

At our centres around the world, we're often (rather sheepishly) asked by clients whether they have to stop smoking "grass", "weed", "cannabis", or marijuana. To be clear, we don't encourage, endorse or recommend the use of any illicit drug, but as long as the smoker avoids mixing their drug with nicotine they're perfectly able to carry on smoking those other drugs once they've quit, using a pipe, a bowl, or hot-knifing it, instead of mixing it with tobacco.

There are three important caveats to this advice:

1. It would be far better, from a health point of view, to find a less toxic way of taking the drug – in tea, for example.

2. Never, ever let the fact that you "get away" with smoking neat joints encourage you to be so confident of your freedom that, at some point in the future, you casually share a joint containing tobacco at a social event. If you do, you'll be smoking again in no time at all. GUARANTEED! Don't do it!

3. Don't use joints as substitutes. If you attempt to replace cigarettes with neat joints, you'll lose your job, your partner, your house, and your whole purpose in life, seemingly without a care in the world! My tongue is firmly in my cheek on this point, but please don't let that detract from this warning; any substitute, of any sort, let alone one containing one of the drugs mentioned, will lead to you smoking again.

If you use these drugs now, and wish to carry on using them once you've quit smoking, then separate their use. Carry on smoking as normal and if you have a joint between now and finishing the book – make sure you have it as prescribed above, i.e. without nicotine.

If you're reading this book in the USA or any other country where it's not the practice to mix "weed" with nicotine then, nevertheless, please adhere to the advice on the previous pages that relates to you.

Most of the smokers who attend our centres indicating they started smoking in their late 20s or early 30s often became addicted to nicotine as a result of smoking joints containing tobacco. At some point, they realize that they're smoking more and more joints, without realizing that it's often the nicotine which they're most addicted to, and nicotine addiction that's driving their "weed" (or whatever) consumption.

We offer one-to-one treatment for cannabis and cocaine, and a host of other drugs, at our London centre, with online treatment via live video-link to anywhere in the world. The first thing we ask those who seek our help is that they separate the drug from the cigarette (when nicotine is involved in the drug taking). It is only then that we can deal with the drug in question.

THE TRUTH ABOUT CASUAL SMOKERS

Casual smokers give the impression of being in control because it suits them to do so. No one wants the world to know they're a pathetic slave. If only all smokers would take their head out of the sand and declare their hatred of smoking, it would be extinct in no time. It's only the illusion that other people are enjoying smoking that makes it difficult to stop.

There is no reason to envy casual smokers for the limited amount of smoking they do. Think about it: you're really envying them for the amount of smoking they *don't* do. Some people who smoke for the first time are lucky and they don't get hooked. The unlucky ones become smokers. Heads you gain nothing, tails you lose everything. It makes you wonder why anyone lights that first cigarette…

Unless you believe that there is a third option, an idyllic middle ground where you can be neither a non-smoker nor a smoker who's hooked for life.

A happy casual smoker. This is the delusion that fools everyone who smokes "just the one".

If this is the type of smoker you would like to be, let me ask you a simple question: why are you not one already? And if you claim to be one, why are you reading this book? Let's get rid of these illusions about casual smokers once and for all.

If I said I could fix it so you could smoke just two cigarettes a day for the rest of your life, would you go for it? Better still, suppose you could control your smoking so you smoked only when you really wanted to. That's a pretty exciting prospect, isn't it? But that's what you already do! Has anyone ever forced you to light a cigarette? Every cigarette you've ever smoked has been because you've chosen to, even though part of your brain wished that you didn't.

So I take it that you'll settle for just the two cigarettes a day. Well, if that's what you want, you can do just that. Who's stopping you? In fact, why haven't you been smoking just two a day for your entire smoking life? Could it be that you wouldn't have been happy smoking just two a day? Of course, you wouldn't. Nor is any other smoker.

Sure, there are plenty of smokers who restrict themselves to smoke just two cigarettes a day. They appear to be in control because they try very hard to give that impression, just as they have to try very hard to limit their smoking… every day… for the rest of their lives. Remember these three facts:

1. The tendency is to smoke more, not less

2. All smokers wish they had never started

3. All smokers lie to themselves as well as to others.

ALLEN CARR'S CASEBOOK:
1. Would you envy someone who
smokes five cigarettes a day?

"A man rang me late at night, desperate to see me as soon as possible. His opening words were, 'Mr Carr, I want to stop smoking before I die.' He explained that he had already lost his legs through smoking, now had throat cancer and had been told that he had to stop or he would be dead within a few months. He said he couldn't go 'cold turkey', so he was cutting down gradually. He had gone from forty to five a day but couldn't cut down any further. I told him to smoke whenever he wanted and come and see me in a few days.

The man began to cry over the phone. He explained it had taken him a year of tremendous willpower and misery to get from forty to five and it had left him a broken man. He spent every minute of every day obsessed with waiting for the few minutes' reprieve when he could have one of his five cigarettes. I booked him into our next available appointment.

Fear keeps smokers hooked and when they've already crippled themselves, they're even more frightened. Cutting down makes you feel more uptight because you have to wait for your fix, and it increases the illusion of pleasure by making each cigarette seem more precious. This all serves to increase the panic and fear, which is one of the biggest barriers to communication.

It took two sessions to convince the man to open his mind, understand the trap and get free. One of the key points for him was the joy of no longer being controlled by the drug. When he was on forty a day, he was hardly even conscious of smoking them, but on five a day his entire life was dominated by cigarettes. Day in, day out, it was sheer torture.

Prior to calling me, he had been to see his doctor, who had prescribed him a chewing gum containing precisely the drug that he was so desperate to kick. If you're imagining some weak man crying his eyes out, you can forget it. He was an ex-serviceman and he was as hard as nails but smoking had brought him to his knees. A few minutes ago, you might have casually envied or even aspired to be a five-a-day smoker. Don't."

All smokers fear they will kill themselves, yet they tell themselves it will never happen to them. They're burying their head in the sand. Millions of smokers each year suffer the trauma of discovering they've made themselves ill by smoking. Not one of them thought it was going to happen to them.

It's amazing how a smoker will buy, for example, a lottery ticket in the hope that they will win. Now, in the main UK National Lottery, the chances of winning the jackpot are one in 45 million. ONE chance, in FORTY-FIVE MILLION! Why do they buy a ticket? The thought process is "Someone's got to win it – IT COULD BE ME!"

Yet tell a smoker that there's a one in two chance that smoking will kill them 10, 20, or 30 years before their time, and what will they think?

"IT WON'T BE ME!"

Think about it. A one in 45 million chance of being a multi-millionaire and we'll not only buy a ticket, but keep our fingers crossed, and check the result with a sense of excitement, expectation, and hope. Yet there's a one in two chance that smoking will destroy us and what do we think? "It won't be me." Can you see the anomaly here?

I'm not telling you this to worry you, and certainly not to scare you. I just want to ensure that you are beginning to see the smoking trap for what it is, and all the amazing, fantastic bonuses you're set to enjoy after Day Four. You don't have to worry about any of this any more.

If you're reading this worrying you might have "done all the damage already", please don't. There is not an illness or disease known to man where quitting smoking doesn't dramatically improve the prognosis many, many times over, to quite an extraordinary extent.

ALLEN CARR'S CASEBOOK:
2. The Guilty Solicitor

"Such is the power of the myths around smoking that a highly intelligent person can still take it up after losing both parents to lung cancer. A lady solicitor rang up and insisted on paying for a private session. She had been smoking for twelve years, since her parents died, but had vowed never to smoke more than two cigarettes a day because she was terrified of contracting lung cancer herself.

Most smokers would think that being able to smoke just two a day would be a dream come true. This is part of the myth. We assume that casual smokers are in control. People who knew the lady solicitor thought she was a happy casual smoker in full control. She wouldn't cry or show her fear in their company. Like all smokers, she felt helpless and stupid and put on a very convincing show to conceal her inadequacy. In truth, she was living a nightmare.

For twelve years, she craved nicotine but her fear of

contracting cancer gave her the immense willpower and discipline required to resist the craving for all but the twenty minutes when she was smoking those two cigarettes each day. She hated being a smoker, but kept her hatred to herself out of shame. While other smokers envied her apparent control, she was constantly battling her addiction.

This lady's apparently casual smoking was controlled entirely by fear. Yet she just couldn't bring herself to quit completely. Her self-imposed restriction was her biggest hindrance. The less she smoked, the less likely she was to fall ill and the more precious the cigarette appeared to be. Thus her motivation to quit was diminished and her fear of deprivation increased, making it impossible for her to quit. Only when she was able to understand this and see that those two cigarettes a day were doing absolutely nothing for her whatsoever was she able to stop smoking completely."

The nicotine trap is unrelenting: the more you consume, the more you want to consume; the less you consume, the more you want to consume. It's like tying someone up, so that the slightest movement tightens the rope around their neck.

OCCASIONAL SMOKERS

But what about those casual smokers who seem so cool and relaxed that it's impossible to believe they're suffering? I'm talking about the ones that can go for days without smoking and just have a cigarette every now and then. In the eyes of other smokers, these lucky people really have got their smoking under control. They seem to have been spared the misery of addiction.

The truth is very different and you can unveil it by asking one simple question:

WHAT'S THE POINT?

If they think they're getting some genuine pleasure or crutch from these occasional cigarettes, why wait so long in between? If they don't, why smoke at all?

If you're a heavy smoker who envies occasional smokers, have you ever tried cutting down to one or two a day yourself? If so, what was it like? Every time I ask a heavy smoker the same question they reply that it was hell, or words to that effect.

Smokers who go for weeks without a cigarette don't even suffer the illusion of getting pleasure or a crutch from smoking, they just go through the motions to be part of the company. All smokers started off like that, convinced that they would never get hooked. They're like a fly hovering around the lip of the pitcher plant and they often turn into heavy smokers.

If you think it sounds appealing to only want one cigarette every now and then, wouldn't it be even better never to want one at all? All smokers who restrict their smoking are creating a number of serious problems for themselves:

- They keep themselves physically addicted to nicotine. This keeps their brain craving cigarettes.

- They wish their lives away waiting for the next fix.

- Instead of smoking whenever they feel like it and partially relieving their craving most of the time, they force themselves to suffer constant mental aggravation and conflict.

- They reinforce the illusion that smoking is enjoyable.

Cutting down increases the illusion of pleasure because the longer you crave nicotine, the more marvellous it feels when you relieve the craving. "What's so bad about that?" you might ask. Because it's not genuine pleasure, it's relief from discomfort, like wearing tight shoes for the pleasure of taking them off. The only way to increase the illusion of pleasure is to increase the discomfort.

No smoker enjoys that discomfort – and casual smokers have to endure it longer than other smokers. Casual smoking is rarely sustainable. The addiction makes you want to scratch the itch, not suffer it, and the tendency is to smoke more and more.

Casual smoking is a terrible form of slavery. You're constantly using willpower to restrict the amount you smoke and constantly thinking about whether or not you will allow yourself to smoke. Get it clear in your mind:

YOU DON'T CONTROL YOUR SMOKING; IT CONTROLS YOU

Most smokers know from experience that cutting down doesn't help you quit. On the contrary, it usually leaves you more addicted. It's much easier to escape the trap by stopping outright. There's no need for half measures. Even if you switched to vaping for the rest of your life, why would you want to when you can be free of the whole filthy nightmare?

STOPPERS AND STARTERS

Casual smokers and occasional smokers have the worst of both worlds: they can neither smoke when they want to, nor do they have the wonderful joy of being free. The same is true of smokers who are always stopping and starting again.

This type of smoker is also envied by heavier smokers because they appear to have control over their smoking, in the same way that occasional smokers do. Not wanting to appear stupid, they encourage the misconception – but, of course, it's a lie.

Think about it: if these smokers truly enjoy being smokers, why do they keep stopping? And if they don't enjoy being smokers, why do they keep starting again? The answer is very obvious: they don't enjoy being smokers and they don't enjoy being non-smokers either. How tragic! Trapped in a kind of purgatory, repeatedly going through the trauma of quitting and the misery and self-loathing of starting again.

To be a happy non-smoker for the rest of your life you need to achieve the right frame of mind. If you believe you're making a sacrifice you will always feel deprived. If you regard just one puff on a cigarette as a pleasure or crutch, you'll remain vulnerable for the rest of your life.

Easyway makes it easy to quit completely and permanently by helping you to remove any desire to smoke. That doesn't mean you can smoke the occasional cigarette and use the method to get free again. If you feel the desire for "just the one" cigarette then the Big Monster is still alive, you haven't removed the brainwashing and you still believe the myth.

Our mission is to remove your desire to take even a single puff of a cigarette, because if you want one you will want a million. Even if you resist the temptation to have that single puff but merely desire it, you will not be a happy non-smoker. You will be a miserable ex-smoker.

Eventually, when your willpower runs out, you will cease to be a miserable ex-smoker and will become an even more miserable smoker.

And the most miserable smoker of all is…

THE SECRET SMOKER

Secret smokers can't even pretend that they enjoy smoking. They steal furtive drags when nobody is looking, then try to remove the smell with peppermints, air freshener and other futile means. They're not kidding anyone except themselves.

Does that ring a bell? You tell your loved ones you're going to quit but don't and then start lying to cover it up. Breaking the promise is bad enough but to compound that by lying is the ultimate humiliation.

If you smoke openly you can at least claim that you smoke because you choose to. As a secret smoker you have to admit to yourself that you're a pathetic slave to nicotine. Secret smokers go through life despising themselves. People with great integrity find themselves lying to conceal their shame. They even start believing their own lies, despite the obvious signs: the yellow stains on their fingers, lips and teeth, the smell on their breath, in their hair and on their clothes.

This is what the addiction does to you. When you've tried as hard as you can to cut down or quit and still you find yourself helplessly drawn back to smoking, the confusion, despair and shame make a liar of you. But although you lie to your loved ones and to yourself, underneath you remain acutely aware of the painful truth: you're a slave to nicotine, a miserable, pathetic drug addict.

ALL SMOKERS ARE THE SAME

It doesn't matter what type of smoker you think you are, all smokers have something fundamental in common: they all wish they had never started. You have no reason to envy any of them. They are all victims of the trap from which you are trying to escape. And you're doing well. You are nearly three days in with one day left to complete your escape and eventually to feel the moment of revelation.

Every type of smoker would love to wake up in the morning in the position you'll be in a day from now.

FREE

DAY THREE: CHAPTER FIVE
BURNING QUESTIONS

THIS HAS BEEN THE MOST DEMANDING DAY OF THE FOUR-DAY BOOT CAMP. UNRAVELLING THE BRAINWASHING IS NOT HARD BUT IT DOES REQUIRE COMMITMENT AND AN OPEN MIND. YOU NEED TO DIGEST WHAT YOU'VE LEARNT AND CHANGE YOUR MINDSET FROM ONE OF BELIEVING THAT SMOKING PROVIDES SOME SORT OF PLEASURE OR CRUTCH TO ONE OF TOTAL UNDERSTANDING THAT IT DOES NOTHING FOR YOU AT ALL. AS YOU LOOK FORWARD TO TESTING YOUR NEWFOUND KNOWLEDGE, SOME QUESTIONS WILL ARISE. I'M HAPPY TO ANSWER THOSE.

THE TRUTH ABOUT SMOKING

Congratulations on getting to this point. Most smokers go through their lives oblivious to the understanding that you have gained in the last three days. You are in a very powerful position. Not only do you hold the keys to your prison, you now have the knowledge to use them.

You may already feel absolutely clear in your mind that you no longer have any desire to smoke and you're ready to quit. If so, resist the temptation to skip to the final cigarette. You might miss something vital. If you still harbour some, or even a lot of uncertainty about your ability to quit, don't worry, that's perfectly natural. Take the time and care to complete the book and regardless of whether you can believe it or not at this stage, you'll be a happy non-smoker in no time at all.

As we prepare for your final day as a smoker, let's recap everything you've learned.

There is no pleasure in smoking

There is only the illusion of pleasure. Any perceived enjoyment is merely temporary and partial relief from the empty, insecure feeling of nicotine withdrawing from your body.

That triggers a thought process in your mind that makes you feel more and more deprived and makes the illusory relief appear even greater.

Smoking to achieve that feeling is like wearing tight shoes just to get the relief of taking them off. It's like being grateful to the thief for returning $10 of the $100 he secretly stole from you. Would you be grateful in those circumstances once you discovered what he'd done?

You don't need willpower to quit

You only need willpower when you have a conflict of wills. Remove the desire to smoke and you lose any sense that you're depriving yourself when you quit. Believe that you're making a sacrifice and you will always be vulnerable to starting again.

There is no such thing as an addictive personality

If you think you have addictive traits, it's because you became hooked on an addictive drug, not the other way round. Even if you're convinced that you have an addictive personality or genes – the great news is that you'll still find it easy to get free. This addiction is easy to break when you know how... regardless of genes and personality.

Smoking does not help you concentrate

It actually makes it harder. Nicotine addiction is a constant distraction. The Little Monster starts crying for its next fix as soon as you start withdrawing from the previous cigarette and it becomes impossible to concentrate on anything else until you satisfy the craving.

Smoking does not ease stress

Nicotine addiction is a major cause of stress. The constant desire for a cigarette, no matter how slight, means you are never fully relaxed. Any sense of relaxation you get when smoking is just the partial relief of the discomfort of withdrawing from the previous cigarette and the ending of the mental aggravation it (the Big Monster) causes. It is temporary, and as you stub out the cigarette the discomfort creeps back in. Quit smoking, get free of the Little Monster and your overall stress levels will fall considerably.

All smokers lie

Pay no attention to what smokers say, whether it's about the supposed benefits of smoking or the terrible trauma of quitting. Smokers lie to cover up their sense of shame and helplessness. You know the truth. See through the illusions and fix your mind on the true picture.

Smoking is not freedom

Anyone who argues that the choice to smoke is down to the rights of the individual fails to understand addiction. You don't smoke out of choice; you smoke to feed your addiction. Smoking and vaping control the smoker, not the other way round. It's not freedom; it's slavery.

Screen stars aren't real

The powerful influence of famous role models attracts millions of people to smoking. Over the years, many of those role models have expressed deep regret for their part in promoting the world's biggest killer – often after they have been diagnosed with cancer themselves. The image of smoking portrayed on screen is dishonest – it is not truthful about the smell, the ugly stains, the bad breath, the nervousness, irritability, stress, ill health and slavery. If it was, nobody would be attracted to smoking in the first place.

Substitutes don't work

Replacing cigarettes with another source of nicotine is guaranteed to keep you addicted. Using a substitute to gradually cut down on your nicotine intake actually makes quitting harder. As you restrict your intake, so the sense of deprivation increases and the drug seems more precious. The easy way to quit is to unravel the myth that smoking gives you some sort of pleasure or crutch, remove any desire to smoke and stop completely.

Neither smoking nor vaping keeps you thin

Most heavy smokers are overweight. They are constantly suffering the empty feeling of withdrawal from nicotine, which feels just like hunger. When they're not smoking, they're eating. Neither satisfies the craving for the other. When you quit with Easyway, you recognize that the empty, insecure feeling of withdrawal is not painful, it's the barely perceptible death throes of the Little Monster, and you know that eating won't make it go away. After a few days the Little Monster dies and you're free from the feeling for good.

All smokers are the same

There is no reason to envy other smokers for the amount they do or don't smoke. All smokers are in the same trap, controlled by the drug and constantly fighting the urge to smoke more. If you think you can get away with smoking the occasional cigarette, ask yourself this: "Why would I want to?" If you answer, "Because it will give me pleasure or a crutch," then you haven't seen through the myth. You need to go back and re-read Days Two and Three until it's clear in your mind that

Neither smoking nor vaping does anything whatsoever for you

You need to be absolutely clear on this. Before you smoke your final cigarette, you have to make sure the Big Monster that interprets the cries of the Little Monster as "I want a cigarette" is dead. Otherwise, you will be forever drawing on your willpower to fight the temptation to smoke.

With Easyway, you remove the temptation altogether. When you stub out your final cigarette, you will have no remaining desire to smoke another ever again.

How will I know when I'm a happy non-smoker or non-vaper or non-nicotine addict?

This is the most common question smokers ask when they're attempting to quit. How will I know when I've succeeded? It's natural to ask this question because most smokers will have tried to quit before, using willpower, and will know the feeling of uncertainty that dogs you with that method. People make their own assumptions.

"I'll know I'm a happy non-smoker when…

"…I can go out drinking with my friends or enjoy a meal without wanting a cigarette."

"…I've managed to go a whole day without a cigarette."

"...I feel like a non-smoker."

In each case, the smoker assumes that they will have to get through an initial period of feeling deprived – and they have no idea how long that may last.

With the willpower method, you never know when you've succeeded in quitting because you are constantly waiting for something NOT to happen – the moment when you give in and light up another cigarette. All you can do is hope it won't happen. Sadly, in the vast majority of cases, it happens all too soon.

With Easyway, the uncertainty is removed. You don't have to wait for anything. You become a happy non-smoker the moment you stub out your final cigarette. Killing the Big Monster means achieving absolute certainty that you will never desire another cigarette in your life. This is how a non-smoker feels. They are aware of cigarettes – they may even believe part of the myth – but they have absolutely no desire whatsoever to smoke. The only reason anyone continues to smoke is to relieve the withdrawal pangs created by the previous cigarette.

Once you have this clearly in your mind, it's easy to unravel the rest of the brainwashing and kill the Big Monster. With Easyway, you kill the Big Monster before smoking your final cigarette. With the willpower method, you kill the Little Monster and hope the Big Monster will leave you alone. But as long as the Big Monster remains alive and you believe that there is some pleasure or crutch to be derived from smoking, you will never be free.

THE MOMENT OF REVELATION

Days Two and Three have been dedicated to changing your mindset from one of wanting to smoke to one of moving towards having no desire to smoke whatsoever. Don't worry if you don't think you've moved towards that mindset yet – all will become clear.

Achieving this change of mindset is a simple process of unravelling the brainwashing step by step, examining the myths that surround smoking and dismantling them one by one. If you think there are still some illusions that you haven't quite seen through, go back to the relevant chapter and read it again.

If you have any questions, please feel free to contact your nearest Allen Carr Centre. They'll be happy to spend a few minutes with you on the phone answering any queries that might have arisen. Check *www.allencarr.com* for details.

That said, I fully expect Day Four to handle every single query or concern that you might have.

While killing the Big Monster is a simple process, there is nothing unusual or stupid about having to go over certain points more than once. It's much better that you achieve complete certainty over each point than rushing to the end. There is also nothing unusual or stupid about believing that quitting smoking is one of the hardest things to do. We are all brainwashed into believing that, smokers and non-smokers alike, and the efforts of other smokers to quit through willpower appear to confirm it. You may even have proven it to yourself with your own previous efforts.

And so you may have reached this point, fully understanding everything you've read, yet still feeling apprehensive about your own ability to quit. Somewhere in your mind you suspect that it can't be this easy – there must be a major hurdle waiting to trip you up.

THE ONLY THING THAT CAN STOP YOU NOW IS YOUR OWN DISBELIEF

Seeing through illusions means believing the evidence of your own eyes. Set aside everything you have ever been told about smoking and look at it logically. If you have understood everything about addiction, about the trap and the myths that keep smokers believing they're getting some pleasure or crutch from cigarettes, then all you have to do now is allow yourself to believe.

THERE IS NO CATCH

It really is that simple. Once you understand beyond all doubt that the cigarette, far from relieving the empty feeling, causes it, you have already removed the cause of panic at the thought of quitting.

You are on the brink of achieving something remarkable. It could be the most life-changing thing you've ever done. You now know that everything you've ever been led to believe about the perceived benefits of smoking, or the difficulty involved in quitting, was a lie. The moment when all this knowledge falls into place and all doubt is removed is the moment when the Big Monster dies. We call it "the moment of revelation". For some people it is a huge thrill, like a blinding flash of light, a sudden realization of the truth and the opening of a prison door. For others, it is little more than the completion of a circle, a logical conclusion that enables them to calmly stub out their final cigarette and get on with life as a happy non-smoker. For some, it doesn't happen until a few days or even weeks after they've quit. It suddenly dawns on them, maybe after an event or incident that might have caused them to smoke in the past, "WOW! I'm free! I didn't even think about smoking!"

In either case, don't wait for it to happen while you're reading this book or afterwards; one thing I can assure you of is, you will have that moment. Enjoy it.

WILL THE GOOD TIMES STILL ROLL?

As a smoker, you believed that cigarettes provided you with a pleasure and a crutch. No doubt you had your "special" cigarettes, such as the first one you smoked after a meal. These are the cigarettes smokers fear they'll miss the most and they formulate the notion that the good times will cease to roll if they're not able to cap them with a cigarette.

The notion of "special" cigarettes is a smoker's fantasy. One smoker who came to see Allen Carr explained that the one thing holding him back was the thought that he would never be able to sit outside a café in Paris, watching the crowds go by, sipping a glass of wine and smoking a Gauloise cigarette. On further investigation it transpired that the man had never even been to Paris, let alone been in that situation. It was all a fantasy, probably something he'd seen in a movie. Yet he couldn't bear the thought of never doing it. He was moping for a myth.

If you're fortunate enough to find yourself in Paris on a sunny day, take a seat outside a café, order a drink, watch the crowds go by and see how it feels. You'll find it has all the charm and appeal anyone could imagine and is all the better for not having to choke yourself to death at the same time.

Those so-called "special" cigarettes only seem special because they come after a prolonged period of abstinence – sleep, eating, a game of sport, etc. Think back over your smoking years and try to remember a single cigarette that made you think, "I'm so glad to be a smoker." I'm sure you'll remember many that stirred the opposite feeling, cigarettes that made you cough and struggle for breath and made you feel utterly miserable.

You will no doubt remember occasions too when you felt utterly miserable because you weren't allowed to smoke, and how relieved you were when you finally got to light up, but that's different. If you're honest, you'll find that the only occasions when you're truly aware of your smoking are when you want a cigarette but can't have one, or when you're smoking one but wish you didn't have to. If you continue believing that you can't enjoy certain situations without smoking, then you won't.

Part of the process of changing your mindset is recognizing that smoking does not enhance good times, it taints them. You need to turn your belief around so that this is clear. Analyse the situations I've described above to understand why the cigarette appears to enhance them but actually does the opposite.

As a happy non-smoker, you will enjoy the good times in life more. You will feel more relaxed without nicotine withdrawal, you won't have the anxiety of making sure you're stocked up with cigarettes, you won't have to worry about spoiling the enjoyment of other people by blowing foul smoke and breathing stale breath in their face... plus, you'll have the immense satisfaction of knowing that you are free from the awful slavery of the nicotine addict.

WILL THE HARD TIMES HURT MORE?

Let's be honest about this, no one goes through life without some hardship and pain. It is perfectly normal. Our aim is not to protect you from ever suffering again; that would be utterly unrealistic. But by becoming a non-smoker, you will be more resilient when fate turns against you.

Smokers believe cigarettes provide a crutch – something they can lean on to help them through life's hardships. A typical scenario is a car breakdown. It's late at night, pouring with rain, you're on the most dangerous part of the road, your phone has no signal and all the other drivers on the road are hurrying past at high speed, rather than stopping to see if they can help. Some of them are even tooting at you, as if you've chosen to park your car there for the fun of it.

It's a miserable, forlorn situation and a smoker would reach for a cigarette, thinking it will give them some respite from the stress and misery. The challenge arises the next time you're in this situation, after having become a non-smoker. Miserable and angry, you think to yourself, "At times like this I would have had a cigarette." It's a crucial moment and you must be prepared for it.

Look back at the last time you faced such a crisis and you lit up. Did smoking solve your problem? Did you have a sudden change of mood and stand there in the rain happily thinking, "Never mind the car or the fact that I'm wet and miserable, I've got this marvellous cigarette!"? Or were you still utterly miserable? If you think at that time you were consoled by the cigarette, that's the thief giving you $10 of the $100 he stole. A non-smoker in that situation can focus on the situation and doesn't have to worry about running out of cigarettes or whether they can smoke or not.

When people who have quit with the willpower method find themselves in these situations, they start to mope for a cigarette. They don't realize that smoking, far from helping the situation, actually makes it worse by adding extra layers of stress to an already stressful situation.

As part of your change of mindset, make sure you accept that there will be ups and downs in life, just as there are for other non-smokers, and that if you think a cigarette will help at such times you will be moping for an illusion, grasping for something that does not exist and creating a void. Be absolutely clear – removing cigarettes from your life does not leave a void.

CIGARETTES DON'T FILL A VOID; THEY CREATE ONE

Ex-smokers who don't understand this suffer the misery of turning good days into bad days and making bad days worse. With Easyway, you turn your mindset around so you can do the opposite. You won't miss cigarettes and you will enjoy life more. You will be better equipped to deal with the natural stresses and anxieties that life throws up. And no matter how bad life gets, you will always be able to pick yourself up with the thought

YIPPEE!

I'M FREE!

ARE YOU READY?

It's not just crisis situations that can trigger the thought of smoking. Happy occasions like Christmas, weddings and holidays are also likely to stir memories of your smoking days. It's nothing to worry about. All you have to do is be prepared for them.

Ex-smokers who quit with the willpower method are easily caught off guard. The temptation to smoke in social situations like weddings can be overwhelming if you still believe that you will be missing out if you don't have a cigarette. Take some time to think about the occasions and moments in life that might be a trigger for you and then prepare your response in advance.

In any situation when your thoughts might turn to smoking, instead of thinking, "I used to have a cigarette in this situation," think, "Isn't it marvellous! I no longer have to smoke. I'm free!" That way you will turn any association between the occasion and smoking to your advantage, reinforcing the truth that smoking does absolutely nothing for you and that you have no need or desire to smoke.

We have spent the last two days replacing illusions with truths. All you need to do now is convince yourself that you don't just understand those truths but that you believe them wholeheartedly. Remember, once you see through an illusion you cannot be fooled by it again.

There is nothing waiting to trip you up. As you lie in bed tonight, you should feel an incredible sense of excitement. You are on the brink of a fantastic achievement. Like a prisoner who knows that release awaits them tomorrow, think about all the wonderful benefits that freedom will bring: better health, more money, greater self-esteem, less stress, better concentration, no fear, no guilt, no slavery. Or put another way

TOTAL HAPPINESS

Recap everything that you've learned so far. Go over all the myths and make sure you are completely clear, seeing things as they really are, not through the distorted lens of addiction and brainwashing. If you have any lingering doubts, go back to the relevant chapter and re-read it. Tomorrow is a very big day – the day you smoke your final cigarette and become a happy non-smoker for life. Congratulate yourself on reaching this point. Millions of smokers would love to be in the position you're in now, holding the key to your own prison cell. Ask yourself a couple of last questions:

DO I WANT TO USE THE KEY?

OR DO I WANT TO REMAIN A SLAVE FOR THE REST OF MY LIFE?

There can be only one answer, the one all smokers would give if they possessed the knowledge that you now have. Sleep well... and prepare yourself for

FREEDOM

CHECKLIST

I understand that:

- ○ **All smokers lie to themselves and to others.**
- ○ **Smoking is not freedom; it's slavery.**
- ○ **I don't control smoking; it controls me.**
- ○ **There is no pleasure in smoking.**
- ○ **Smoking is just the process smokers go through to get their drug.**
- ○ **Smoking is not a habit; it's drug addiction.**
- ○ **The tendency will always be to smoke more.**
- ○ **Smoking does not make you thin.**
- ○ **The next cigarette could be the one that kills me.**
- ○ **Smoking does not ease stress.**
- ○ **Cigarettes don't fill a void; they create one.**

THE BIGGEST DAY OF YOUR LIFE

Welcome to the most important day of your life! I do not exaggerate! Perhaps you feel you've had more important days: the day you were born perhaps; the day you fell in love; got married; had your children. These are all momentous, happy days that change your life – but today is the day you save your life.

Today you will smoke your final cigarette, or e-cigarette, or take your final dose of nicotine, and you will do so with the absolute certainty you will never want more. Just think what that means – you will never again suffer the slavery and degradation of being a nicotine addict.

Everybody has different things that they look forward to most about being free from smoking. Some look forward to feeling healthier, free from the wheezing and coughing, the headaches and nervous fidgets, more energetic and vibrant. Some look forward to having more money to spend on genuine pleasures.

Some can't wait to tell their family and friends, bringing an end to all the guilt and secrecy, and regaining their self-respect. Some just want to be free from the slavery of nicotine addiction.

As I've said throughout the book, there are lots of marvellous reasons for stopping smoking, but the most important reason of all is this:

FREEDOM FROM THE SLAVERY

All smokers know the arguments for not smoking and can't understand why they find it so hard to quit. They don't understand the nature of the trap they're in and the fact that they're addicted to nicotine. And so they feel enslaved by some unknown force that compels them to keep smoking against their better judgement.

You do understand the trap and you know that the only reason you have continued to smoke is because of nicotine addiction. Now you have the key to unlock your chains and be free. Remember, you're doing this for yourself. It is you who is being freed from slavery and all you need to think about is your own journey. Everything else will fall into place.

Today I will lead you to the thrilling moment when you smoke your final cigarette, reinforce your commitment to never smoke again and walk free from the nicotine trap for good. Allow yourself to feel very excited. Remind yourself of everything you stand to gain and of everything you now know about the smoking myth and the brainwashing that creates it. Focus on those two monsters inside you and prepare to unleash your vengeance on them for all the misery they've caused you.

Are you ready? Let's go!

THERE IS NOTHING TO FEAR

AS YOU APPROACH THE MOMENT WHEN YOU SMOKE YOUR FINAL CIGARETTE, IT'S NATURAL TO FEEL BUTTERFLIES IN YOUR STOMACH AND MISTAKE THIS FOR THE FEAR OF SUCCESS. REMEMBER, FEAR PLAYS A VERY VALUABLE ROLE IN YOUR SURVIVAL TOOLKIT, BUT THE FEAR OF BEING A NON-SMOKER IS COMPLETELY IRRATIONAL.

SMOKING DOES NOTHING FOR YOU

When you first picked up this book you were under the impression that you derived some pleasure or crutch from smoking and you were looking for help in overcoming your need for that pleasure or crutch. As you've read through the book, you have turned your understanding of smoking on its head, so you should now be very clear on a number of facts that are the complete opposite of what smokers believe, such as:

SMOKING OR VAPING OR ANY OTHER FORM OF NICOTINE CONSUMPTION DOESN'T RELIEVE YOUR CRAVING; IT CAUSES IT

NICOTINE DOESN'T EASE STRESS; IT IS A MAJOR CAUSE OF STRESS

YOU DON'T CONTROL SMOKING; IT CONTROLS YOU

At Easyway, we are often asked, "If smoking does nothing for you whatsoever, why tell us to keep smoking until the final cigarette?"

It is a sensible question. Again, you need to turn it on its head. It is important for you to keep smoking as you read the book, not because of what smoking does for you but for what happens to you when you don't smoke.

The Big Monster tells you "I want a cigarette" as the nicotine from the previous cigarette withdraws from your body. If you're not allowed to smoke, you become fidgety and distracted. This inability to concentrate is caused by cigarettes, so we need to make sure that you aren't distracted from the task in hand because of that. Once you've had your final cigarette, your concentration will no longer be disturbed by cigarettes, but until that time it's important that you continue to smoke.

There is another reason for continuing to smoke, vape, or take nicotine as you read the book, and that is to test the illusions, myths and misconceptions for yourself. For example, the taste test.

Exercise: **THE TASTE TEST**
Your first exercise on Day One was to pay attention to every sensation involved in smoking a cigarette, e-cigarette or vape, particularly the taste and smell as you suck the smoke down into your lungs. Let's repeat that exercise now. Light a cigarette, or "vape up", take five or six deep puffs and ask yourself precisely what you're enjoying about it. If you're honest, you'll find it's absolutely nothing.

We find that smokers and vapers become more and more reluctant to undergo these exercises as they go through the method. They become impatient to ditch nicotine and get to the point where they can say with pride, "I am a happy non-smoker," or "I am free of nicotine."

If that's how you feel right now, great. It shows that your desire for nicotine is shrinking, the Big Monster is dying, if not already dead, and you are well on your way to quitting permanently. If you don't feel that way, please don't worry: I only have good news for you.

All I ask is that you are patient. You are very nearly there but it's essential that you make absolutely sure that the Big Monster is dead.

REAL vs IMAGINARY FEARS

Nicotine addicts don't need to be told that it's a mug's game. They are perfectly capable of weighing up the advantages and disadvantages and concluding that they would be much better off not being addicted, yet they also know that the force that compels them to carry on is very real. Moreover, they know what it feels like when they don't respond to that force.

No one wants to spend the rest of their life feeling the way a nicotine addict feels when they can't have their drug and this is why they fear the thought of becoming free. What they don't realize is that nicotine causes that feeling and the only way to be completely rid of it is to stop taking the drug.

Fear is the force that keeps you in the trap. It feeds on all the brainwashing and myths that you've been bombarded with from an early age. It's important to recognize that this fear is caused by the addiction to nicotine, as distinct from the genuine, instinctive fears that form a vital part of your survival toolkit.

The instinctive fears that protect us from fire, falling, drowning, etc., are all perfectly logical. The fear of not being able to smoke is completely illogical. It is a fear based on your imagination, which is clouded by illusions. People who don't smoke don't suffer with it at all.

THE FEAR OF BEING FREE OF NICOTINE WAS CREATED WHEN YOU STARTED SMOKING

For smokers still caught in the nicotine trap, however, this fear is very real. The willpower method advises them to fight through the fear, when it's obvious that what they really need is to have their eyes opened to the fact that the fear is not founded in reality. Easyway removes the fear by showing you that there is nothing to fear, there is no sacrifice, no deprivation, no pain or discomfort whatsoever. Smoking does absolutely nothing for you whatsoever and when you stop, all the things you think you're going to miss evaporate.

But you don't have to wait until you are a non-smoker to make the fear disappear. You can easily remove it by approaching the subject with an open mind and trying to be relaxed, logical and rational. Then you will be able to see the truth through the illusions and you will have no reason to fear life without smoking.

NO NEED FOR A SAFETY NET

Once they realize that it's just fear that prevents them from stopping, some smokers try to set their fear aside by telling themselves that they can always start smoking again if they're finding it hard – quitting doesn't have to be final. This is a big mistake. If you start off with that attitude you're very likely to be dragged back into the trap.

High wire artists who don't use a safety net may be adding an extra element of drama to their act, but there is more to it than that. During practice, they will use a safety net because they are not yet certain that they have perfected their routine; however, by the time of the performance they are so certain of their act and their ability to carry it off that the presence of a safety net would actually be a hindrance – sowing a seed of doubt in their mind, which can throw them off balance.

The same applies with your own great act – escape from the nicotine trap. In order to walk free easily, painlessly and permanently, you must have complete certainty about what you're doing. Telling yourself you can always take up smoking again if you're struggling is like quitting with a safety net.

The whole point of a safety net is that it should go unused. The great thing about becoming free is that there's no danger. You're not going to fall and hurt yourself; nothing bad is going to happen. You simply don't need a safety net any more than you would need a handrail to walk across an empty room.

The certainty you need is in your hands. Perhaps you think nothing in life is ever certain. After all, the chances of being hit by a meteorite are infinitesimally small, yet there remains a possibility that it could happen. OK, that's true. But here's the difference. If a meteorite is going to hit you, there is absolutely nothing you can do about it. It's not your decision, whereas smoking a cigarette is entirely your decision. As long as you don't make that decision, you can be absolutely certain that it won't happen.

Q: WHY DOES ANYONE EVER LIGHT UP A CIGARETTE?

A: BECAUSE THEY WANT TO

Wait a minute! At the beginning of this chapter I restated the fact that you don't control smoking, smoking controls you. Doesn't this go against the above statement that you only smoke because you want to?

This brings us to the key to quitting with Easyway. As a smoker, you choose when you smoke every single cigarette. Nobody else forces you to do it. Yet it's what controls the choices you make that makes the difference. As a smoker, it's nicotine addiction that controls your choice to smoke.

Free from addiction, it's easy to make the choice not to smoke. It's in your hands. When you put out your final cigarette, you can be absolutely certain that you will never smoke another cigarette again. All you have to do is make sure you are never again struck by the thought "I want a cigarette". You can achieve this by making sure you have three vital facts ingrained in your mind:

1. Smoking, vaping, or any nicotine product does absolutely nothing for you whatsoever. You must understand why this is. That way you will have no feeling of deprivation.

2. You don't need to go through any transitional period (often referred to incorrectly as the "withdrawal period") before the craving goes completely. Craving is mental, not physical and yours will be gone by the time you've finished reading this book and the physical withdrawal is so slight it's hardly perceptible.

3. There is no such thing as "one cigarette" or "the occasional cigarette". Never think in terms of one cigarette; think of a hundred thousand cigarettes, a lifetime's chain of filth, disease, and misery.

MAKE YOUR CHOICE

A lot of smokers find it hard to believe that they have a choice about whether to crave cigarettes or not. They are trapped by the misconception that you either crave something or you don't, and there's nothing that you can do about it. Fortunately, they're wrong. Your body will continue to experience nicotine withdrawal for a few days after quitting as the Little Monster goes through its death throes, but that doesn't mean you have to be miserable or that you have to crave a cigarette.

How you respond to the Little Monster dying is completely up to you. The physical feeling is very slight, the mildest feeling you can imagine, no more alarming than, out of the corner of your eye, noticing a bit of fluff on your shoulder. At first it might surprise you, but after a moment you'd simply respond by gently brushing the fluff away. You wouldn't panic nor would you worry about the next piece of fluff that might land on your shoulder.

It's the Big Monster in your mind that reacts to that mild feeling by creating a mental process which, in turn, causes more troubling physical feelings. The great news is that, once you've changed your mental reaction to the mild physical feelings, the thought processes become enjoyable rather than bothersome.

The discomfort you've experienced in the past has been based on the following thought process triggered by the mild withdrawal feeling:

"I want a cigarette! I can't have one! AGHHH!"

If there is no pleasure, benefit, or crutch obtained from smoking, then you won't want a cigarette. True? Of course, it is.

If you don't want a cigarette, then you won't have that "AGHHH!" feeling. True? Of course, it is.

If you understand that, then you're on the verge of becoming a happy non-smoker.

If after today you ever feel that you're having that "I want a cigarette" thought, please don't worry. After years of smoking, it wouldn't be surprising. Remember, it's just like spotting a bit of fluff out of the corner of your eye on your shoulder. Just brush it off and don't let it send you into a panic.

All it means is that you momentarily forgot that you quit; it doesn't mean you want to smoke. No more than nearly taking a wrong turn on your way home from work towards your old apartment means that you want to move out of the amazing apartment you moved into recently. It just takes some time for our brains to get used to our new situation.

The willpower method encourages smokers to fixate on the craving by making it the focus of their resistance. They have to use their willpower to try to avoid thinking about smoking. If you've ever made a conscious effort to NOT think about something, you'll know what a futile exercise this is. Let's try it now.

Exercise: **WHAT'S ON YOUR MIND?**

This is a very simple exercise. All you have to do is not think about elephants.

That's right, don't think of elephants.

You probably weren't thinking of elephants anyway but

I bet they're on your mind now. How can they not be? Your mind does the same thing when you try not to think about smoking. It becomes almost impossible to think about anything else!

With Easyway, you can choose to brush off the Little Monster completely. It's really not hard – the feeling is so slight. Or you can choose to rejoice in the feeling – after all, it signals the death of a mortal enemy. This is a very important point. Many smokers are convinced that cigarettes are their friend, their crutch, their source of confidence and courage, even part of their identity. They fear that quitting will hit them like losing a close friend and maybe even a part of themselves. That's why these smokers become whining ex-smokers. But their behaviour is very different to genuine grief.

When you lose a close friend, you mourn, you suffer shock and there's a huge sense of loss at the initial tragedy. But, to an extent, you recover from this shock and get on with life. The loss leaves a void in your life that can never be filled, you rightly keep your special memories of your friend alive, and look back fondly, but you have no choice other than to accept the situation and eventually you do.

But you're not losing a friend today. As a friend it would be most peculiar; it stinks, controls your every move, steals your money, won't leave you alone, and is trying to kill you. That's not a friend. It's an enemy!

When you rid yourself of a mortal enemy, there is no mourning. On the contrary, you can celebrate right from the start… and continue celebrating for the rest of your life, rejoicing every time the thought of that evil monster enters your mind.

So get it perfectly clear in your mind: the cigarette is not your friend and never has been. It has done absolutely nothing for you, ever, but it has harmed you constantly since the day you first started. It is your worst enemy and you are sacrificing nothing by cutting it out of your life, just making marvellous positive gains.

So if you're wondering when the craving will go, the simple truth is:

THE CRAVING GOES WHENEVER YOU CHOOSE

You could spend the next few days, and possibly the rest of your life, continuing to believe that cigarettes were your friend and wondering when you'll stop grieving for them. Do that and you'll feel miserable, the craving may never go and you'll either feel deprived for the rest of your life or, more likely, you'll end up smoking again and feeling even worse.

OR

You could recognize the cigarette for the evil enemy that it really is. Then you need neither crave a cigarette, nor wait for anything to happen. Instead, whenever the thought of smoking enters your head, you can rejoice: "Yippee! I'm a non-smoker!"

REPROGRAM YOUR BRAIN

During the first few days after your final cigarette, the Little Monster will be crying out, sending messages to your brain that it wants you to interpret as "I want a cigarette".

Now you understand the true picture, instead of feeling compelled to smoke, or feeling uptight because you can't, you know there's no need to panic. Pause for a moment. Take a deep breath and simply brush it away as if it was a piece of fluff on your shoulder.

Over these four days, we have reprogrammed your brain to enable you to see the true picture and to respond to the various triggers with a logical mindset, instead of the illogical, addicted mindset that you began with.

Previously your mind interpreted the withdrawal pangs of the Little Monster as "I want a cigarette", because it had been filled with misinformation convincing it that a cigarette would satisfy the empty, insecure feeling. But now your brain is equipped with different information – the truth – and you understand that, far from relieving that feeling, cigarettes caused it.

So just relax, keep your mind open, and accept the feeling for what it is – the Little Monster fading away. In this frame of mind, these become moments of real pleasure rather than moments of struggle.

Now you need to prepare your mind for other triggers that will occur, particularly during the first few days after your final cigarette. You might find, for example, that you forget you've quit. This can happen at any time. It often occurs first thing in the morning when you're coming around from sleep. You find yourself thinking, "I'll get up and have a cigarette." Then you remember that you've quit and you may feel shaken, worried that your mind is relapsing into the mindset of a smoker.

A similar thing may happen when you're socializing. Suddenly there's a packet of cigarettes thrust under your nose and you instinctively reach out to take one. Then you catch yourself and withdraw your hand. "Aha!" say the smokers around you, "I thought you'd quit." They're almost gleeful, as if their main aim is to catch you out and drag you back into the trap.

Both these situations can be disconcerting and doubts can creep in if you're not prepared, so make sure you're ready in advance. There will be times when you forget that you're a non-smoker and something will trigger your old thought process. This is actually a good sign. It shows that you're not obsessed with smoking or not smoking; you're just getting on with life like any other non-smoker. It is not a sign that part of you still wants a cigarette. Prepare yourself for these situations so you see them coming and are ready to remain calm and react with total confidence, laughing off your action and thinking, "Isn't it great? I don't need to smoke any more. I'm free!" These situations are no more concerning than taking the wrong turn to your old apartment shortly after you've moved.

Smokers will envy you because every single one of them would love to be like you.

FREE FROM THE FILTHY NIGHTMARE

Other triggers could be after a meal, when having a drink, after sex... any of the occasions when you used to think the cigarette was "special". Although you have freed your mind from the illusion that these cigarettes were special, the association between these occasions and smoking can linger as a habitual reaction that turns your thoughts to smoking. Again, see these moments as a cause for celebration. Rejoice that you are now able to enjoy and genuinely cherish these moments rather than interrupt the fun to have a cigarette and choke yourself to death. This interruption of relaxing moments (after a meal), social moments (with a drink), or moments of pure unbridled passion and pleasure (after sex) occurs whether someone smokes cigarettes, or vapes, or uses any other nicotine products. Being free from that is priceless. If your partner smokes – don't worry – cut them some slack and let them take their smoking breaks when they need to. Do your best not to make them feel bad about it and they'll see how easy you've found it to be free and will, in time, be likely to emulate you.

Once you're prepared, you won't be tripped up. Like the high wire artist, you will have absolute certainty and every little wobble will only add to the excitement of the act. Where you once had fear, you will have an incredible sense of freedom – the freedom of being a happy non-smoker.

TAKING CONTROL

ALL SMOKERS HAVE THEIR OWN POWERFUL REASONS FOR WANTING TO QUIT BUT THEY ARE AFRAID OF WHAT THEY'RE GOING TO MISS IF THEY BECOME A NON-SMOKER. WHEN YOU QUIT, AND REALIZE YOU'RE NOT MISSING ANYTHING, YOU APPRECIATE THE GREATEST GAIN OF ALL: ESCAPE FROM THE SLAVERY.

ONE SIMPLE STEP

Smokers start out with the belief that they are in control. Even after years in the trap, they still convince themselves that they smoke because they enjoy it. Deep down, they know this isn't true, but they can't understand the real reason they continue to light up. It feels like an unseen force keeps compelling them to smoke, even though they wish they didn't have to. That unseen force is fear created by addiction.

As I've explained, it is not a genuine fear – i.e., it is not based in reality and so it is not logical – but to the smoker it feels genuine enough. It is the fear of life being unbearable without the cigarette.

Smokers go through their entire smoking lives controlled by this fear, slaves to addiction. And because they don't understand it they close their minds to it and make up flimsy excuses for smoking –

excuses like "I like the taste" and "It helps me relax" or "It helps me concentrate".

This is the Big Con that keeps all smokers in that miserable prison camp. It's an ingenious prison camp. It has no walls, no gates, no guards, nothing, yet the prisoners are kept captive by their own beliefs and fears, which are instilled in their minds by a tyrant called

ADDICTION

Not only does each prisoner act as their own jailer, they work together to keep everyone else imprisoned too, by spreading the fears instilled in them by the tyrant. Nobody knows exactly what would happen if they tried to escape, but they are sufficiently afraid of it to choose to stay in the camp, even though the tyrant has made it quite clear that he intends to kill them! They're so afraid of how bad things might get that they don't address how bad things already are.

Get this clear in your mind: nothing bad is happening here today. You'll be missing out on nothing other than a lifetime of misery.

If you harbour slight doubts about cigarettes helping you to be happy, helping you to cope with sadness, or helping you to relax, concentrate, handle stress, enjoy a drink, enjoy a meal, or a break from work, then see it the way it really is.

What does a smoker or vaper have to do when they're happy?

What does a smoker or vaper have to do when they're sad?

What does a smoker or vaper have to do when they want to relax?

What does a smoker or vaper have to do when they need to concentrate?

What does a smoker or vaper have to do if they need to handle stress?

What does a smoker or vaper have to do if they want to enjoy a drink?

What does a smoker or vaper have to do if they want to enjoy a meal?

What does a smoker or vaper have to do if they want to enjoy a break from work?

Smokers have to smoke! They don't do it through choice on any of these occasions. They have no choice. They have to smoke or vape day in, day out, every single day of their lives. They're incapable of doing anything without a cigarette or e-cigarette before, during, or after it. The addiction makes it impossible for them to even grieve properly without one. Can you think of anything more pathetic than that? These aren't arguments for smoking; these are the biggest arguments against it.

That's the way it is. And the way it always will be. Nothing will ever change the life of a smoker or vaper. Except two things: stop living or GET FREE! Smokers have to go through life as miserable, humiliated slaves.

There are evil regimes that have preyed on human fear in this way throughout history. The tyrant of nicotine addiction is no less evil. But there is one key difference: if you had tried to escape the clutches of one of the tyrants the human race has thrown up so often, the consequences could have been dire.

Escape the clutches of nicotine addiction and nothing bad will happen to you at all. On the contrary, you will make many wonderful gains. You don't need to plot any daring escapes. There are no walls or fences to overcome, no guards training their guns on you. All you have to do is stop being controlled by the Big Con and step out of the prison camp.

It's that easy.

If you can imagine being in that prison camp, crammed in with all the other smokers, all suffering, sick, enslaved and lying to yourselves and one another – and then imagine taking that one simple step to the outside, where the air is clean, your head is light and your vision is clear, that is the sense of freedom and happiness you can look forward to as a non-smoker. That is freedom from slavery and it is the most wonderful of all the wonderful gains you stand to make by stopping smoking.

LAME EXCUSES

We all have our pride. Feeling controlled, like a slave, is a terrible blight on a person's self-esteem. All smokers suffer the indignity of having to see themselves as slaves. After a short time in the trap the excuses change from deluded lies like "I enjoy the taste" to defensive and negative arguments:

"I can afford it."

You can probably afford heroin too; why don't you take that? The average smoker spends over $140,000 (£100,000) on cigarettes in their lifetime. Smokers don't avoid taking heroin because they can't afford it; they avoid it because they regard it as a filthy drug that enslaves its victims and leaves them as pathetic, sick addicts.

So what's the difference?

"I haven't noticed any deterioration in my health."

So you're going to wait until you get ill before you consider quitting? Or are you denying that smoking is bad for you? As a vaper, you instinctively know that you're doing yourself harm.

"I haven't got any other vices."

So you're only smoking or vaping because you think you need a vice? That suggests you know it's bad for you and you're only doing it for that reason and that you genuinely choose to do it. Where's the logic in that? Drinking stagnant pond water is bad for you too. Why not "choose" to do that instead? Or are you suggesting that smoking is more pleasant than drinking stagnant pond water? Really? How? Both taste and smell foul. At least pond water is free and it's not addictive. The same goes for vaping. Would you drink pond water as a vice if it was flavoured with caramel? Of course not.

Aside from the lack of basis to these excuses, they aren't so much reasons for smoking as reasons for not stopping smoking. A double negative.

Compare that to the sort of reasons someone might give for taking part in a genuine pleasure, like playing sport, going to the cinema or dancing.

"I enjoy the camaraderie."

"I love the way it captures my imagination."

"It transports me out of the present moment."

"It makes me feel amazing."

These are powerful, positive reasons for pursuing genuine pleasures, not lame excuses for not stopping doing them.

This highlights the difference between life as a smoker and life as a non-smoker. As a non-smoker you don't need lame excuses. There is no sense that you're doing something stupid that you need to justify somehow. You can hold your head up high and speak the truth with enthusiasm and joy.

I'M A HAPPY NON-SMOKER. I'M FREE!

The Big Con keeps smokers trapped in the prison camp by closing their minds to the truth. Easyway helps smokers take the easy step to freedom by opening their minds to the truth. And the most simple truth of all is this:

YOU DON'T NEED TO BE A SLAVE

Non-smokers who have never smoked find it hard to understand why smokers need to have this simple truth pointed out to them. They have never been in the prison camp so they don't know what it's like in there. There are plenty of truths in life that are kept from us by industries that make gains from our ignorance: the junk food industry, for example. Plenty of non-smokers become obese by eating junk food. They too have missed a simple truth. They are no more or less stupid than smokers; if you're not told the truth, how are you supposed to know?

I was lucky enough to discover the simple truth that I smoked because I was addicted to nicotine, not because I enjoyed it or derived some sort of crutch from smoking. Until that moment I had found it impossible to quit. That simple truth enabled me to walk free with one simple step.

Quitting smoking means taking control and control comes with the realization that you do have a choice. You don't need to remain a slave, you can walk free, you won't miss smoking, you will enjoy life more, you will cope better with stress, you won't have to go through some terrible trauma to escape. This is the truth.

ALL SMOKERS WANT TO QUIT

This is another truth concealed by the Big Con. All those poor souls in the prison camp secretly wish they could escape, but they don't admit it for fear of the consequences. If they admitted it, then they would have to go ahead and try to escape, and that prospect frightens them. They've been told that escape is painful and miserable at best, impossible at worst. So they keep their secret desire for freedom to themselves and carry on doing the tyrant's work, spreading the myth that they smoke because they want to.

But there is plenty of evidence that all smokers want to quit. Take the enormous industry for nicotine substitutes. Who's buying all the patches, gum, pills, snus, vaping kits, etc., if it's not smokers who don't want to smoke? It's a fact that more and more vapers are now attending our centres. They're either smoking and vaping or, in the case of a few, just vaping. If life as a vaper was that great, why would they pay us to seek our help? If you're a vaper and resistant to this argument, ask yourself why on earth you're reading this book. It's because you're fed up of the control and slavery of being an addict and simply want to be free.

Then there are all the smoking parents who implore their children not to smoke. If you genuinely believe there's some benefit in smoking, why discourage your children? The truth is that all those smoking parents wish they didn't smoke and the last thing they want is to drag their children into the same trap.

Surveys have recorded that 70% of smokers say they want to quit. I can add that the other 30% just won't admit it. They would rather perpetuate the impression that they're in control by saying, "I smoke because I choose to and I have no desire to stop," rather than admitting, "I smoke because I'm a miserable addict and I would give anything to quit but I don't have the willpower."

Easyway has grown into a worldwide organization because of the universal demand among smokers for a cure that will help to stop them smoking. The vast majority of the people who attend our centres around the world or read our books or use our video-on-demand service do so, not as a result of advertising and marketing, but because they know a smoker for whom the method worked. More often than not, they know many smokers for whom the method worked.

ALLEN CARR'S CASEBOOK: FREE CIGARETTES FOR ALL!

"In my first book, *The Easy Way to Stop Smoking*, I told a story about offering so-called confirmed smokers – those who have no intention of stopping – free cigarettes for the rest of their life if they gave me the money they would spend on cigarettes in just one year. The book has sold over 12 million copies yet no one has ever taken up the offer. Why not? Because it would be a life sentence. All smokers and vapers think short term. They all plan to stop… soon.

Have you noticed how all the smoking paraphernalia has changed? There was a time when we used to buy each other expensive lighters, cigarette cases or ashtrays as special gifts, such as a 21st birthday or a wedding gift. These days you rarely see such things. Smokers prefer disposable lighters. They don't want to see their smoking in the long term."

Every smoker and vaper or addict of any other nicotine product, either openly or secretly, would love to be in the position you'll be in when you finish this book. Most smokers are strong-willed and it frustrates them immensely that they can't gain control over their smoking. You are about to discover how wonderful it feels to be free from that frustration, that constant feeling of being controlled. It's a marvellous feeling, just to stand on the outside of that prison camp and look back at those poor smokers, not with envy or a sense of deprivation but with genuine pity, as you might look at any other drug addict. The greatest gain from quitting smoking is not so much the health or the money but the end of the self-loathing, no longer despising yourself for being a slave to something you detest.

BACK TO HEALTH

No smoker or vaper in their right mind could possibly deny that smoking is bad for your health. They can push the thought to the back of their mind, bury their head in the sand, but every single one of them knows the proven health risks that come with smoking and the quite obvious health risks of vaping, or snus, or dip, or anything else. Most smokers will know first hand how smoking robs you of energy, leaves you coughing and choking, unable to run more than a few yards without wheezing and gasping for breath. It also destroys your sex drive, which is ironic, given that so many people start smoking because they think it will make them more sexually attractive.

These are among the more minor effects. Hanging over all smokers and vapers, and those who love them, is the terrifying dark cloud of critical illnesses like lung cancer, heart disease, arteriosclerosis, emphysema, angina and thrombosis. It's no secret that all these diseases have been closely linked to smoking and smokers know it better than anyone. Every packet carries a stark health warning and a photograph of some repulsive condition caused by smoking. Every smoker, even the most foolish, knows that they're putting their health in terrible danger.

The tobacco companies are obliged to put warnings on cigarette packaging. It's supposed to shock smokers into reconsidering their decision to smoke. It doesn't work. If shock tactics did work, I would have no hesitation in using them on you. But you don't need to be told about the vile things that smoking can do to your body. Smokers are aware of the health risks and the more they are forced to think about them, the more they retreat into their prison and seek comfort in their little crutch. Such is the cunning nature of addiction:

SMOKERS SEEK COMFORT IN THE VERY THING THAT'S KILLING THEM

The reason I am focusing now on the health impact of smoking or vaping is not to shock you but to highlight another burden you'll be shedding when you quit – the burden of fear. The tug-of-war of fear that all smokers suffer is like being trapped in a burning building. You have two frightening options: stay inside the burning building or jump. Most smokers opt to stay inside, hoping to be rescued. Only when the fear of dying in the flames becomes greater than the fear of jumping will they make their move.

Smokers are afraid to jump because they believe that life as a non-smoker will be lacking some vital ingredient. But they are afraid to continue smoking too because they know it's likely to kill them. If you don't stop, the chances of you dying as a direct result of smoking are greater than 50 per cent. Yet, just as if they were in a burning building, smokers won't jump until it becomes absolutely essential. They instinctively put off what they see as "the dreadful day", hoping that some other miracle will come along and save them.

But the nicotine trap is a far more subtle danger than a burning building, and so the smoker has an additional problem over the person in the burning building. In a burning building, you cannot close your mind to the danger. It's clear and present and you know that if you stay put the fire will get you eventually.

For the smoker, the danger is not immediately apparent and until they are diagnosed with some terrible disease, smokers will delude themselves: "It won't happen to me" or "I'll stop before it gets to that stage – I'm not a complete idiot."

There seems to be no pressing need to solve the problem today and so smokers typically choose to put it off.

Non-smokers find it difficult to understand why smokers and vapers are prepared to take these risks for the dubious pleasure of breathing poisonous fumes into their lungs. But non-smokers aren't caught up in the tug-of-war of fear. They know how easy it is to live without cigarettes and they have no desire to smoke, so all their attention is focused on the fear of remaining in the burning building. To the non-smoker the solution is obvious...

GET OUT NOW!

The great thing is that you're not having to leap from a burning building. You're taking one easy step to freedom. It's not a case of a soft landing. There isn't any "landing" at all. Turn the key and you're free.

But smokers can be very strong-willed and this, combined with the delusion that it won't happen to them, drives them to carry on.

Smokers twist the odds to suit their excuses. They're told they could win the lottery at odds of 45 million to 1 and they believe, "It could be me." Then they're told they have a 1 in 2 chance of dying from smoking and they convince themselves, "It won't be me." When tragedy does strike and they succumb to the dreaded disease, they turn the logic around: "There's no point stopping now. I've left it too late."

But even though smokers are mostly in denial about the dire consequences of smoking, they still sense they're being stupid. If they had to face up to the fact that it was going to cost them $140,000 (£100,000) and the next cigarette could be the one to trigger cancer, even the illusion of pleasure would disappear and the whole process would become intolerable.

ALLEN CARR'S CASEBOOK: THE LEGLESS STAR

"If you were warned that you were going to lose your legs if you didn't stop smoking, would you stop? Most smokers respond to this question with a quick 'Yes, of course I would!' Yet remarkably many smokers don't heed the warning and end up having to have their legs amputated. All smokers need to understand that they could make the same mistake – nicotine addiction can close your mind to even the starkest of warnings.

A large proportion of smokers are not even aware that smoking can result in the loss of limbs. Buerger's disease is a form of thrombosis caused by smoking, where the blood vessels in the legs become damaged, preventing the flow of blood. Clots form and the tissues begin to die from a lack of oxygen. If the tissue damage is not halted, the legs have to be amputated.

I remember this happening to poor Arthur Askey, the music hall comedian. He had to have his legs amputated as a direct result of his smoking and still he didn't quit. You can imagine him thinking, 'I've lost my legs – what else have I got to lose?' When I heard this news I was still a smoker and I remember thinking, 'At his age, are legs really essential?' Like him, I was making my own warped evaluation of the situation. 'You can live without legs but cigarettes are essential.' I honestly regarded cigarettes as more important than my own legs! Such is the effect of addiction on the brain. If you ever question just how evil a tyrant nicotine addiction is, this case should leave you in no doubt."

The more miserable and afraid a smoker becomes as they slide further into the trap, the more they turn to their "little crutch" for comfort. Each cigarette drags you further and further down. You suffer the triple low of nicotine withdrawal, the debilitating effects of smoking and the fear of knowing you've lost all control. Eventually you fall so low that you become resigned to your fate. The addiction takes away your instinct for survival. The Big Monster has become your master and it will only be finished with you when you die.

GET YOUR RETALIATION IN FIRST

Non-smokers don't suffer any of the lows that smokers do. All this misery, all this fear, can be ended quickly, easily, painlessly and permanently by killing the Big Monster and stopping smoking or vaping. No longer will you have to block your mind to your failing health. Quite the opposite, in fact; you will rejoice in the feeling of your health being restored.

You could be one of those smokers or vapers who hasn't noticed any deterioration in your health yet, or you could be a smoker who has already suffered health problems as a result of your smoking – it doesn't matter. All smokers are walking through a minefield and disaster could strike at any time.

Perhaps you take the philosophical approach that we've all got to die some time so what's the point of worrying about it? The problem is that, as a smoker, you're not going through life free of such worries. As a smoker you have more to worry about than a non-smoker. You chose to read this book because you're worried about it.

You worry about dying enough to look both ways before you cross the road, don't you? Your attitude isn't one of ignoring the bus hurtling towards you as you step off the kerb because "Well, we've all got to go some time!", is it?

It's time to say goodbye to the worries of life as a smoker once and for all. Let me turn that philosophical approach on its head: if you never know how much life you have left, why spend that life burdened with unnecessary worries or even just the inconvenience of being addicted? Wouldn't it be better to enjoy every moment, free from worrying about your health and feeling like a slave?

THE TRUTH ABOUT WITHDRAWAL

WHEN SMOKERS FEAR THAT QUITTING WILL BE PAINFUL, THEY'RE THINKING ABOUT THE WITHDRAWAL PERIOD, WHEN THEY FIRST STOP TAKING THE DRUG AND ANY REMAINING TRACES OF IT DRAIN OUT THEIR SYSTEM. THEY'VE BEEN BRAINWASHED TO BELIEVE THAT THE PHYSICAL EFFECTS OF WITHDRAWAL ARE TRAUMATIC. THE TRUTH IS VERY DIFFERENT.

NO PAIN, HUGE GAIN

I've described the withdrawal from nicotine as a mild, uneasy, empty, slightly insecure feeling. I've also stated that the only reason a smoker lights up is to relieve that feeling, and that eventually that feeling causes a mental process during which the Big Monster creates the "I want a cigarette! I can't have one! Aghhh!" feeling.

WITHDRAWAL IS 1% PHYSICAL AND 99% MENTAL

The physical sensation of withdrawal is so mild as to be almost imperceptible.

Smokers spend a lot of time planning to make sure they never find themselves in the dreaded situation of having no cigarettes. It's a thought that can create panic long before their cigarettes run out. How often have you been out at night and calculated that you'll be awake for another four hours, but only have enough cigarettes left to last an hour? The realization creates panic, which intensifies as you smoke the last cigarette in your packet. Even though you're smoking and nicotine is flowing into your body, the panic feels like withdrawal pangs. That's the Big Monster.

ALLEN CARR'S CASEBOOK: THE PANIC-FREE SMOKER

"Most of the smokers who come to our centres nod knowingly when I refer to 'that panic feeling' you get when you know your supply of cigarettes is running out. But there's sometimes one who shows no recognition at all. 'I'm sorry,' he says, 'I have no idea what you're talking about.' The rest of the group stare at him in surprise.

These looks turn to incredulity when I later remark that smokers will smoke camel dung rather than nothing, and the panic-free smoker says, 'I can't agree with you. If I couldn't get my own brand, I wouldn't smoke anything.'

Is he being honest? We know that all smokers have to lie to themselves but when they come to one of our seminars we generally find that they welcome the chance to be honest and purge their conscience. So is the panic-free smoker the exception that proves the rule?

Not at all. The panic-free smoker is always a heavy smoker and the reason he doesn't know the panic feeling is because he has always made sure to avoid it. The panic-free smoker is so frightened of suffering that panic feeling that he takes every precaution to make sure he never gets low on cigarettes.

And while he believes it must be his chosen brand or nothing, he has never tested that belief. The panic-free smoker is neither lying nor telling the truth. He just hasn't discovered yet what it feels like to be denied cigarettes. Every smoker who is prevented from smoking feels that panic.

I used to panic when I got down to my last few packets! I wasn't happy playing a round of golf unless I had three full packs on me. I could only smoke 40 per round at a push, so why the need for three packs? It all stemmed from an occasion when I used to carry two and I dropped one pack in a puddle. The cigarettes were soaked and ruined. So I learned from my mistake and made sure I always carried three packs to cover every eventuality."

The panic of withdrawal is all in the mind. It's the Big Monster that ties you in knots, makes you fidget and sends you racing to the shop in the middle of the night to make sure you're well stocked up. There is no physical pain. The physical sensation that arouses the Big Monster is minuscule.

It's uncertainty that causes the panic. Earlier in the book we looked at the example of students sitting an exam without being distracted at all by the craving for a cigarette. It's the same situation when you board a plane. You have certainty. You know you're not going to be allowed to smoke for the next few hours so you stop worrying about it.

It's when you want a cigarette and feel you should be doing something about it that the fidgets start and the panic sets in.

Exercise: **TEST YOUR PAIN THRESHOLD**

We put up with a lot of pain in life: headaches, stiffness, sore feet, cuts and knocks. From an early age we learn to cope with these pains without throwing a tantrum. Much of the time we suffer in silence, reluctant to inflict our problem on anyone else. Our capacity to cope with pain is higher than you might think.

Try it now. Dig your nails into your thigh and gradually increase the pressure. You'll find you can endure quite a severe level of pain without feeling any sense of panic or fear. That's because you're in control. You know the cause of your pain and you know it's not going to become intolerable.

Now imagine that it wasn't you causing the pain but that it had just come on without any explanation. You have no idea what caused it or how long it might last. Now imagine that pain was in your head or chest. You would begin to panic straight away. It's not the pain that causes the panic, it's the fear created in your mind by uncertainty.

We have spent the last four days clearing your mind of illusions and myths and replacing them with the certainty that smoking does nothing for you whatsoever and you will not miss it at all. When you achieve that certainty about your decision to quit, the minuscule physical feeling of withdrawal doesn't induce fear and panic because you know exactly what's causing it and that it will be gone within a matter of days.

The feeling is the Little Monster dying and you don't even have to wait until it's dead to start enjoying life as a happy non-smoker.

Whenever you feel that tiny sensation, rejoice in the knowledge that you're killing your mortal enemy and making your escape to freedom.

TRAUMATIC TALES FROM THE BIG CON

You have probably heard accounts from smokers who have tried to quit and reported that they went through some terrible trauma. You may even have suffered that trauma yourself. A quick internet search throws up a pretty unappealing list of the symptoms of nicotine withdrawal:

- headaches

- coughing and sore throat

- nausea and intestinal cramping

- tingling hands and feet

- sweating

- weight gain

- anxiety

- irritability

- insomnia

• difficulty concentrating

• depression

Every one of these symptoms is a result of the mental panic that sets in when you try to quit with the willpower method. We've already discussed most of these symptoms, from weight gain down, and you should be clear that they are not caused by <u>not</u> smoking, they are caused by smoking. Depression, difficulty concentrating, insomnia, irritability, anxiety and weight gain are all psychological conditions. The first five symptoms are indeed physical but they are the physical manifestation of the intense stress that you put yourself under when you try to quit with willpower.

People who quit with willpower are taking a leap into the dark. They don't know what it takes to quit, let alone whether they have what it takes. They have no idea how long they'll need to draw on their willpower before their craving goes. They don't even know how they'll know whether they've succeeded in quitting or not. All this uncertainty is created by the belief that they're making a sacrifice. "How long can I cope with feeling deprived?" No wonder they feel anxious as soon as they put out their final cigarette! They feel like they're jumping off a burning building with a blindfold on and waiting for the worst <u>not</u> to happen.

It's the stress and anxiety that cause the headaches, nausea, sweats and other physical symptoms of withdrawal. Take away the stress and the physical symptoms go too. Be aware too that not every smoker who quits with the willpower method suffers these symptoms. Most find that the withdrawal period is actually much less severe than they expected.

You're ahead of the pack – you already know that you have absolute certainty about what you're doing. By the time you begin to feel any slight physical feeling, you already know that you have no need or desire to smoke another cigarette in your life. The fact is you probably won't even notice any physical feelings. Certainly nothing more alarming than spotting a piece of fluff, out of the corner of your eye, on your shoulder.

HOW TO APPROACH WITHDRAWAL

After you put out your final cigarette your body will continue to experience withdrawal from nicotine for a few days. You have a choice about how you handle this period. The one thing you shouldn't do is try to close your mind to the almost imperceptible physical feeling. Try to ignore it and it will start to nag away at you. You have no reason to ignore it. Let's just recap what's going on.

When you lit your first cigarette you created an evil Little Monster inside your body, a parasite that feeds on a powerful poison called nicotine. As soon as you stop smoking and cut off the supply of nicotine, you have done the one thing required to purge yourself of that evil monster.

From this moment the Little Monster begins to die. In its death throes, it will try to entice you to feed it. Create a picture in your mind of this vile little parasite writhing and squirming and enjoy starving it to death.

Keep this image in mind and you will ensure that you don't mistake the feeling for "I want a cigarette". Focusing on the feeling will help you to see it for what it really is. Be aware just how slight the feeling is – an empty, insecure feeling that makes you fidget a bit.

Remind yourself that this feeling was caused by the last cigarette. It may not be a pleasant feeling but it's not intolerable either. Far from it. You could easily live with it. After all, you lived with it every day when you were smoking.

The only difference now is that instead of responding to the feeling by lighting a cigarette, you are responding by doing nothing. As you brush away that piece of fluff you can say to yourself, "YIPPEE – I'M FREE!"

The monster that would have happily destroyed you is now being destroyed by you. Very soon you will be free of any trace of the Little Monster. The only thing that can prevent that from happening is if you respond to its death throes by smoking a cigarette.

NOTHING TO WAIT FOR

Nicotine is a fast-acting drug; most of it leaves the body in a matter of hours. You might be aware of the final traces of it leaving your body for a few days.

For smokers who quit with willpower, the period after the Little Monster dies can be a dangerous time. Having started out obsessed with not being allowed to smoke, they suddenly realize that time has gone by and they haven't thought about smoking. This typically happens after about three weeks, or just over a couple of weeks after the end of the withdrawal period.

Everything the smoker hoped for appears to have come true. They have managed to go three weeks without smoking and it seems they're not even missing it. Wow! It wasn't that hard after all. This is cause for a small reward. And what possible harm could it do to reward themselves with just one cigarette?

If they're foolish enough to light one they'll find it tastes unusual and gives them no illusion of pleasure. Remember, the only reason any smoker thinks the cigarette gives them pleasure is because it partially relieves the symptoms of withdrawal from the previous cigarette. The nicotine from the previous cigarette in this case has long passed out of their system so there is nothing to relieve.

The fact that the cigarette does nothing for them gives them extra confidence. But they've put nicotine back in their body and soon they will feel the withdrawal symptoms again. One little voice will be saying, "That tasted awful," but another will be saying, "Maybe, but I'd like another one." They'll exercise their self-control and resist having another one immediately. They don't want to end up on the hook again so they allow some time to pass.

They feel like they're in complete control but already their willpower is being undermined. The next time they're tempted they can now tell themselves, "I smoked last time and didn't get hooked, so what's the harm in having another?"

Ring any bells?

Before long they're right back in the trap, cursing themselves for their weakness and resigning themselves to a life of addiction.

The fact is, most people who use willpower to quit experience discomfort for months afterwards. They might have killed the Little Monster, but the Big Monster is what causes all the unpleasant symptoms. It is their response to a thought process, no longer triggered by nicotine withdrawal, but triggered by something reminding them that they used to smoke.

People who quit with the willpower method are always watching the clock, always chalking off the days, always feeling like they deserve a reward. With Easyway, there's no sense of marking time and no need for a reward because you don't feel like you're depriving yourself of anything. In fact, you're rewarding yourself from the moment you stub out your final cigarette.

WITH EASYWAY, FREEDOM IS THE REWARD

So by the time the Little Monster dies, you will already be getting on with life as a happy non-smoker and you probably won't even notice the withdrawal symptoms, let alone the fact that they've stopped.

The point is that there is absolutely nothing to fear from the withdrawal period after you quit. You don't have to wait to get through it or behave any differently when it's over. All you have to do is keep in mind that the withdrawal symptoms are so slight as to be almost imperceptible and that they signify that something wonderful is happening.

THE JITTERS

Soon you will smoke your final cigarette ever. The thought of this moment and the freedom from nicotine addiction is incredibly exciting and the thrill can make you feel jittery, nervous and impatient. You might mistake these feelings for panic but you can easily dispel any confusion by reminding yourself of everything you know and understand and asking yourself what possible reason you have to panic. Nothing bad can happen by stopping smoking. Only good can come of it.

Be aware of your reasons for feeling so excited. The tyrant of nicotine addiction has dogged you for too long and now you are about to be rid of it. In just four days you have unravelled all the brainwashing that kept you imprisoned and miserable and very soon you are going to complete the simple step to freedom. From tomorrow you will start to feel physically and mentally stronger. You will have more money, more energy, more confidence and more self-respect.

You stand on the brink of a magnificent achievement. Has it been hard getting to this point? Have you found it painful? Or are you now convinced that it is possible to quit smoking easily, painlessly and permanently, without relying on willpower or using substitutes?

If so, you're ready to prepare yourself for the ritual of

THE FINAL CIGARETTE
(OR E-CIGARETTE, OR ANY DOSE OF NICOTINE BY ANY MEANS)

YOUR FINAL CIGARETTE

AND SO THE MOMENT HAS ARRIVED. YOU STAND ON THE BRINK OF BECOMING A HAPPY NON-SMOKER – COMPLETELY FREE FROM NICOTINE – A MARVELLOUS ACHIEVEMENT THAT WILL BRING YOU TREMENDOUS BENEFITS. ALL THAT'S LEFT IS FOR YOU TO COMPLETE THE RITUAL OF THE FINAL CIGARETTE OR DOSE OF NICOTINE. I'LL SPECIFICALLY INSTRUCT YOU EXACTLY WHEN YOU SHOULD DO THAT.

WHY ARE YOU DOING THIS?

That may strike you as an odd question at this late stage but it's a question many smokers ask themselves as they face the prospect of smoking their last cigarette. It's important to check that you are quitting for the right reason. There are many good reasons for not smoking – health, money and guilt about your loved ones and dependents, for example – but these reasons alone are not enough. If they were, nobody would continue to smoke. You need to be clear that you are quitting because…

THERE IS ABSOLUTELY NO REASON TO CONTINUE TO SMOKE

To the non-smoker, this statement seems glaringly obvious, but for nicotine addicts it's possible to go through life without ever realizing this simple truth: that smoking does nothing for you; it gives you no genuine pleasure or crutch and you will not miss it. Allen Carr's Easyway has changed the lives of countless smokers by opening their eyes to the reality of the situation. When the penny drops, the feeling of relief is fantastic.

It is also essential that you have not made the decision to quit for the benefit of someone else. Many smokers say they want to quit for the sake of their children or their partner. If you do that you will feel that you are depriving yourself and sooner or later you will be tempted to "reward" yourself with just one cigarette. That one cigarette will be enough to set the whole vicious circle in motion again.

You are quitting for the best reason of all: your own happiness. It's you who is getting free, you who is rediscovering the genuine pleasures in life, you who is shaking off the shackles of slavery. As a smoker, you lose your grasp of many of the feelings that make life a joy: feeling healthy, energetic, guilt-free, unstressed, in control, happy. As a non-smoker you will rediscover all these feelings and you will wonder how you ever feared life without cigarettes.

Quit for the simple, selfish reason that you'll enjoy life so much more as a non-smoker. All the other specific things involved – the health benefits, release from the slavery, saving of money, freedom from guilt and fear – are just fabulous extra bonuses for you to enjoy.

Smoking traps you in the slavery of addiction. It twists your perception of reality and fills your head with myths and illusions that keep you in the trap. Continue to smoke and it will eventually kill you, but there will be no pleasure along the way.

Some people die from doing dangerous things that they find exhilarating. Climbing, sky-diving, hang-gliding and motor racing, for example. They choose that way of life and they accept that it might result in their death because to them the thrill is worth the risk. They believe in the sentiment "die doing what you love".

Some smokers adopt the same attitude to smoking, but they're deluding themselves.

There are no thrills to be had from smoking. There is no pleasure at all; it was all just a confidence trick. Is that really a feeling worth dying for? And if you did, could anyone honestly say you died doing what you love?

Smokers and vapers, in fact all nicotine addicts, hate it and wish they could be rid of it. There is nothing more miserable than being dragged into an early grave by nicotine addiction. Despite all the bravado, all of nicotine's victims know they're doing something stupid and if they could find an easy way to quit they would.

Happily for you, you have found an easy way to quit. You are now equipped with all the knowledge you need to escape from the nicotine trap easily, painlessly and permanently.

CHOOSE YOUR MOMENT

A lot of people reach this point in the method feeling that they already have no need or desire to ever smoke again and ask whether it's essential for them to go through the ritual of the final cigarette or having the final dose of nicotine. If you don't feel that way, don't worry, even if you feel sceptical. You're in for a fabulous surprise.

The ritual is important.

This is a momentous occasion, a huge achievement in your life and one that you will always look back on with a sense of pride and elation. It's important to mark the occasion indelibly. The final cigarette or dose of nicotine is your opportunity to focus one last time on the vile reality of smoking and then draw a line under it. That said – if you haven't smoked or taken nicotine for a few days, there is no need for you to go through this ritual. Just confirm to yourself that you've already taken your final dose of nicotine when I prompt you to light your final cigarette or take your final dose, and vow never to let it enter your body again.

So all that's left is for you to choose your moment. You may not have realized it, but you chose your moment when you first picked up this book. It's designed to be read over four days, enabling you to make the transition from unhappy smoker to happy non-smoker in under a week. So when you picked up the book you made the decision that you would become – or at least hoped to become – a non-smoker four days later.

That time has arrived. There is no reason to put it off.

If it took you less than four days or more than four days to read the book – don't worry. This time, right now, is right for you.

Most attempts to quit smoking are timed to coincide with a particular occasion. New Year's Day is the classic example. New Year, new start. Sadly, attempts to quit on New Year's Day have the lowest success rate of any specific day.

Have you ever tried quitting on New Year's Day? You've smoked so much over Christmas that you're feeling sick of it. Your motivation to quit is high and the New Year seems like the perfect time to make a clean start. So you go through the ceremony of smoking one final cigarette as the clock strikes midnight on New Year's Eve and throw the rest of the pack into the fire.

So far, so good, but then a few days pass by and the excesses of Christmas are forgotten about, your health has improved because of your abstinence from smoking, but the Little Monster is crying out for its fix. The motivation for not smoking has gone, you're feeling strong and, because you don't understand that smoking will do nothing but guarantee the fidgets keep returning, you take the offer of a cigarette. It feels good to relieve the craving, so soon you're smoking another, and another.

Specific days like New Year's Day or a birthday are meaningless when it comes to quitting. They crystallize the motivation to quit, but the effect doesn't last. The feeling of deprivation replaces the desire to quit and we soon find ourselves making excuses to smoke again. Having started smoking once more, we're left with a miserable sense of failure and a reinforced belief that quitting is hard.

Then there are those occasions that we had always told ourselves would be our cue to quit, like a health scare. The shock is often enough to make us bin the cigarettes immediately, but after the initial shock come the stress and anxiety, two feelings that typically drive us to our little crutch. As long as you believe that smoking will help to relieve your anxiety and stress, it's inevitable that you will smoke again before long.

Some smokers choose a time when they can get away from the usual temptations, such as their annual holiday or a quiet time on the social calendar. The trouble with this approach is that it leaves a lingering doubt: "OK, I've coped so far but what about when I get back into the usual routine?"

If finishing this book just happens to coincide with one of the "special days" I've mentioned above, don't worry, you'll succeed in spite of that, rather than because of it.

You need to be certain that you have no need or desire to smoke whatever the circumstances. Don't change your lifestyle: go out and enjoy social occasions, enjoy meals and handle stress from the start.

When you've killed the Big Monster you have no need to give yourself time to adjust. You can start enjoying life as a happy non-smoker the moment you stub out your final cigarette.

You made the decision to stop smoking the moment you picked up this book. The time has come.

YOUR TIME TO STOP IS NOW – JUST A FEW MOMENTS AWAY

YOUR CHECKLIST

I'm sure that you have absolute certainty about your reason to quit and about the truth that there is no reason whatsoever to continue smoking or vaping or using nicotine in any form. You may not yet be able to imagine just how great you're going to feel when you get free but you should be feeling the excitement of something marvellous about to happen, like a parachute jumper standing in the open door of the plane. The wonderful truth is, there isn't even an ounce of danger in this instance.

A few butterflies are completely understandable. You are taking a big leap but you're not leaping blind. You are completely certain that what you're leaving behind is nothing but misery, degradation, filth and slavery. I can assure you that the feeling once you've stepped out towards freedom is nothing short of incredible. Nothing bad is going to happen; only a marvellous, exhilarating taste of freedom.

As a final confirmation that you're completely ready, take a look through the **RATIONALIZED** checklist and make sure you have no doubts about any part of it.

R Rejoice!
This is a momentous day. There is nothing to give up but there are many marvellous gains to make.

A Advice
Smokers and non-smokers alike offer it all the time. Ignore it if it conflicts with anything you've learned in this book.

T Timing
Why wait to get free? The ideal time to quit is now.

I Immediate
There is nothing to wait for when you quit with Easyway. You become a happy non-smoker the instant you stub out your final cigarette.

O One Cigarette
There is no such thing as "just the one". One cigarette is all it takes to drag you back into the nicotine trap.

N Never Again
This is the absolute end of your addiction. Never again will you feel the need or desire to smoke.

A Addictive Personality
There's no such thing. You became an addict because you took an addictive drug. You can just as easily become a non-addict.

L Lifestyle
There is no need to change it to avoid smoking situations, unless you want to, of course.

I Intake
Never again subject your body to anything containing nicotine. The drug is the tyrant – how you take it is irrelevant.

Z Zero Sacrifice
There is nothing you're missing out on.

E Elephants
There's no need to avoid thinking about smoking. Try to shut your mind to it and it will become your obsession.

D Doubt
Have none. You are making the most rational decision you've ever made.

Use the word "RATIONALIZED" to remind yourself of everything you know so that you never doubt your decision to quit and never again succumb to the feeling of "I want a cigarette".

Exercise: **YOUR FINAL CIGARETTE**

On Day One I asked you to smoke a cigarette, paying careful attention to every aspect of the process. I'd like you to repeat that exercise now. I would like you to light your final cigarette now please. Likewise if you use e-cigarettes go ahead one last time. The same goes for snus, dip, or any nicotine product.

What does the cigarette look and feel like as you take it out of the packet? And how do you feel? Hold the cigarette under your nose and take notice of how you feel as you sniff the tobacco. How is your heartbeat?

Continue applying this level of attention as you place the cigarette between your lips, light it, inhale that first drag of foul smoke and blow it away from your face and eyes. How does it smell? How does it taste? What is the sensation on your tongue? In your throat? In your nose? In your lungs? How does the cigarette look between your fingers?

Do the same if you're using e-cigarettes or any other nicotine product. Observe what's involved in consuming it. Analyse it as you do so.

If you're smoking, look at the filter tip. Notice the discolouration appearing already.

As the cigarette burns down, remind yourself that this

is one of those rare occasions in life when you are losing nothing and gaining so much. There is no price to pay for this joy, you won't feel any deprivation because you're not "giving up" anything. You're ridding yourself of a deadly enemy. So rejoice.

As you reach the end and stub out the cigarette, look at it in the ashtray and see how filthy and pathetic it looks. Be aware of the taste it has left in your mouth. Now close your eyes and make a solemn vow that you will never smoke again. Hold that thought. Never again will you have to subject yourself to the filth and degradation. Do the same if you use any other nicotine product.

Now open your eyes, remove all traces of the cigarette and any other cigarettes or nicotine products you may have left over and get on with life as normal. With the added bonus of

FEELING INCREDIBLE

DAY FOUR: CHAPTER FIVE
STAY FREE

CONGRATULATIONS! YOU ARE NOW A HAPPY NON-SMOKER AND A HAPPY NON-NICOTINE ADDICT TO BOOT! AS YOU BEGIN YOUR NEW LIFE, THESE SIMPLE TIPS WILL HELP TO ENSURE YOU ARE NEVER TRICKED INTO FALLING BACK INTO THE TRAP. DON'T WAIT FOR ANYTHING. YOU ARE ALREADY A NON-SMOKER, A NON-ADDICT. YOU BECAME ONE THE MOMENT YOU GOT RID OF THAT FINAL CIGARETTE, E-CIGARETTE, OR OTHER NICOTINE PRODUCT. YOU'VE CUT OFF THE SUPPLY OF NICOTINE AND UNLOCKED THE DOOR OF YOUR PRISON.

Accept, that while having nothing to do with having quit nicotine, you will have good days and bad days. That's all part of the stresses and strains of life. However, because you will be stronger physically and mentally, you'll enjoy the good times more and handle the bad times better. Don't ever be tempted to blame a bad day at work or with the kids on the fact that you've quit smoking.

Be aware that a very important change is happening in your life. Like all major changes, especially those for the better, it can take time for your mind and body to adjust. If you feel different or disorientated for a few days there's no need to worry. Just accept it. Feel it. A sense of quiet. A sense of peace. It might seem a little weird for a while. Have you ever seen a movie when someone has been released from a dark, dismal dungeon? As they emerge into the bright sunshine, and feel the breeze on their cheek, they shield their eyes for a moment. Eventually they stop squinting, open their eyes, and sense their freedom. This is where you are. Enjoy it.

You've quit nicotine, you haven't quit living. On the contrary, you can now start enjoying life to the full. Don't alter your lifestyle in any other way unless you want to anyway. Carry on taking your breaks from work – take "non-smoke" breaks. Why miss out on the gossip and the chat of the smoking area just because you quit?

Do not try to avoid smokers or smoking situations. Go out and enjoy social occasions and handle stress right from the start. If your partner or best friend smoke don't avoid them, don't preach to them, and don't interfere with their smoking. You've been released from a terrible ordeal, have compassion. Soon they'll see how cool, calm and collected you are about the whole thing and their curiosity will eventually overcome their fear of stopping and they'll be tempted into emulating you.

Never envy smokers. When you're with them remember that you're not being deprived, they are. They will be envying you because they will be wishing they could be like you: FREE.

Forget substitutes like patches, gum or vaping kits. You don't need them and they don't help anyone to quit. Even apparently harmless substitutes, such as chewing gum, or eating carrot sticks or candy will cause a problem. You don't need a substitute – you've got rid of a disease, not given something up. Any substitute can create and perpetuate a feeling of deprivation and soon awakens the Big Monster. Enjoy and cherish your freedom without substitutes.

Never be in any doubt over your decision to quit – you know it's the right one. If you find yourself thinking "I want a cigarette", don't panic. The feeling is just a hangover from your smoking days. That's a wonderful moment to remind yourself how lucky you are to be free. A moment when you brush that piece of fluff off your shoulder and smile.

Be prepared for the offer of "just one cigarette" or "just one puff". Keep in mind that one puff on a cigarette is enough to drag you back into the nicotine trap. Remind yourself that you have no need for it and if you're offered "just the one", make sure it triggers the thought "YIPPEE – I'M FREE!" Your brain will soon adjust.

Never carry cigarettes with you or keep them anywhere in your house. If you do, you open the door to doubt and almost certainly guarantee failure. Would you advise an alcoholic to carry a flask of whisky in his pocket? That said, if your partner smokes or vapes that really isn't a problem; you don't need to ban theirs from the house. Understand that there's a huge psychological difference between them keeping their cigarettes or nicotine in the house and you keeping some of yours. Get rid of yours; that's all you need to do.

Don't try to block the thought of smoking from your mind. It's impossible to make yourself not think about something. By trying to you will make yourself frustrated and miserable. The thought of smoking doesn't have to make you miserable; it can be a source of great joy. Instead of allowing your thoughts to stray, "I mustn't have a cigarette," or, "I can't have one," remember how things really were when you were addicted and how they really are now and think,

"YIPPEE! I'M A NON-SMOKER! I'M FREE!"

The idea isn't to be scared of going back to the addiction – it's a case of genuinely celebrating and cherishing your freedom.

One last reminder: don't wait for anything to happen. Don't wait to become a non-smoker or non-addict. You already are one. You became one the moment you went through the ritual of your last cigarette, e-cigarette, or nicotine product.

FINALLY

What you have achieved is incredible but remember, you are not alone. Tens of millions of smokers have quit with Easyway. Don't hold back from telling the world about your achievement. You won't be bragging; you'll be helping to dismantle the Big Con and enable and inspire tens of millions more smokers and nicotine addicts to escape to freedom and happiness.

If you ever have any doubts or concerns or questions that arise please don't hesitate to contact your nearest Easyway centre. Every single one of our therapist team around the globe quit smoking with this method and they're always delighted to hear from anyone who has joined them in freedom.

CONGRATULATIONS!

Lastly, congratulations on being free. Enjoy life, free from the nightmare – the life of a smoker, the life of a nicotine addict.

First Instruction:
FOLLOW ALL THE INSTRUCTIONS

Second Instruction:
OPEN YOUR MIND

Third Instruction:
THINK POSITIVE

Fourth Instruction:
BEGIN, NOT WITH A FEELING OF DOOM AND GLOOM, BUT INSTEAD WITH A FEELING OF ELATION AND EXCITEMENT

Fifth Instruction:
IGNORE ANY ADVICE THAT GOES AGAINST EASYWAY

Sixth Instruction:
HAVE NO DOUBT ABOUT YOUR DECISION TO QUIT

ALLEN CARR'S EASYWAY CENTRES

The following list indicates the countries where Allen Carr's Easyway To Stop Smoking Centres are currently operational.

Check www.allencarr.com for latest additions to this list.

The success rate at the centres, based on the three-month money-back guarantee, is over 90 per cent.

Selected centres also offer sessions that deal with alcohol, other drugs and weight issues. Please check with your nearest centre, listed below, for details.

Allen Carr's Easyway guarantee that you will find it easy to stop at the centres or your money back.

JOIN US!

Allen Carr's Easyway Centres have spread throughout the world with incredible speed and success. Our global franchise network now covers more than 150 cities in over 45 countries. This amazing growth has been achieved entirely organically. Former addicts, just like you, were so impressed by the ease with which they stopped that they felt inspired to contact us to see how they could bring the method to their region.

If you feel the same, contact us for details on how to become an Allen Carr's Easyway To Stop Smoking or an Allen Carr's Easyway To Stop Drinking franchisee.

Email us at: **join-us@allencarr.com** including your full name, postal address and region of interest.

SUPPORT US!

No, don't send us money!

You have achieved something really marvellous. Every time we hear of someone escaping from the sinking ship, we get a feeling of enormous satisfaction.

It would give us great pleasure to hear that you have freed yourself from the slavery of addiction so please visit the following web page where you can tell us of your success, inspire others to follow in your footsteps and hear about ways you can help to spread the word.

www.allencarr.com/fanzone

You can "like" our facebook page here
www.facebook.com/AllenCarr

Together, we can help further Allen Carr's mission: to cure the world of addiction.

LONDON CENTRE AND WORLDWIDE HEAD OFFICE
Park House, 14 Pepys Road,
Raynes Park, London SW20 8NH
Tel: +44 (0)20 8944 7761
Fax: +44 (0)20 8944 8619
Email: mail@allencarr.com
Website: www.allencarr.com
Therapists: John Dicey, Colleen Dwyer,
Crispin Hay, Emma Hudson, Rob
Fielding, Sam Kelser, Sam Cleary,
Rob Groves

Worldwide Press Office
Contact: John Dicey
Tel: +44 (0)7970 88 44 52
Email: media@allencarr.com

**UK Centre Information and
Central Booking Line**
Tel: 0800 389 2115 (UK only)

USA
Denver
Toll free: 1 866 666 4299 /
New York: 212- 330 9194
Email: info@theeasywaytostopsmoking.com
Website: www.allencarr.com
Therapists: Damian O'Hara,
Collene Curran, David Skeist

Houston
Toll free: 1 866 666 4299 /
New York: 212- 330 9194
Email: info@theeasywaytostopsmoking.com
Website: www.allencarr.com
Therapists: Damian O'Hara,
Collene Curran, David Skeist

Los Angeles
Toll free: 1 866 666 4299 /
New York: 212- 330 9194
Email: info@theeasywaytostopsmoking.com
Website: www.allencarr.com
Therapists: Damian O'Hara,
Collene Curran, David Skeist

Milwaukee (and South Wisconsin)
Tel: +1 262 770 1260
Therapist: Wayne Spaulding
Email: wayne@easywaywisconsin.com
Website: www.allencarr.com

New York
Toll free: 1 866 666 4299 /
New York: 212- 330 9194
Email: info@theeasywaytostopsmoking.com
Website: www.allencarr.com
Therapists: Damian O'Hara,
Collene Curran, David Skeist

CANADA
Sessions held throughout Canada
Toll free: +1-866 666 4299 /
+1 905 849 7736
English Therapist: Damian O'Hara
French Therapist: Rejean Belanger
Email: info@theeasywaytostopsmoking.com
Website: www.allencarr.com

UK CENTRES
Birmingham
Tel & Fax: +44 (0)121 423 1227
Therapists: John Dicey, Colleen
Dwyer, Crispin Hay, Emma Hudson,
Rob Fielding, Sam Kelser, Ania Martin,
Rob Groves
Email: mail@allencarr.com
Website: www.allencarr.com

Brentwood
Tel: 0800 389 2115
Therapists: John Dicey, Colleen Dwyer,
Crispin Hay, Emma Hudson, Rob
Fielding, Sam Kelser, Rob Groves
Email: mail@allencarr.com
Website: www.allencarr.com

Brighton
Tel: 0800 389 2115
Therapists: John Dicey, Colleen Dwyer,
Crispin Hay, Emma Hudson, Rob
Fielding, Sam Kelser, Rob Groves
Email: mail@allencarr.com
Website: www.allencarr.com

Bristol
Tel: 0800 389 2115
Therapists: John Dicey, Colleen Dwyer,
Crispin Hay, Emma Hudson, Rob
Fielding, Sam Kelser, Rob Groves
Email: mail@allencarr.com
Website: www.allencarr.com

Cambridge
Tel: 0800 389 2115
Therapists: John Dicey, Colleen Dwyer,
Crispin Hay, Emma Hudson, Rob
Fielding, Sam Kelser, Rob Groves
Email: mail@allencarr.com
Website: www.allencarr.com

Coventry
Tel: 0800 321 3007
Therapist: Rob Fielding
Email: info@easywaymidlands.co.uk
Website: www.allencarr.com

Cumbria
Tel: 0800 077 6187
Therapist: Mark Keen
Email: mark@easywaymanchester.co.uk
Website: www.allencarr.com

Derby
Tel: 0800 389 2115
Therapist: John Dicey, Colleen Dwyer,
Crispin Hay, Emma Hudson, Rob
Fielding, Sam Kelser, Rob Groves
Email: mail@allencarr.com
Website: www.allencarr.com

Guernsey
Tel: 0800 077 6187
Therapist: Mark Keen
Email: mark@easywaymanchester.co.uk
Website: www.allencarr.com

Isle of Man
Tel: 0800 077 6187
Therapist: Mark Keen
Email: mark@easywaymanchester.co.uk
Website: www.allencarr.com

Jersey
Tel: 0800 077 6187
Therapist: Mark Keen
Email: mark@easywaymanchester.co.uk
Website: www.allencarr.com

Kent
Tel: 0800 389 2115
Therapists: John Dicey, Colleen Dwyer,
Crispin Hay, Emma Hudson, Rob
Fielding, Sam Kelser, Rob Groves
Email: mail@allencarr.com
Website: www.allencarr.com

Lancashire
Tel: 0800 077 6187
Therapist: Mark Keen
Email: mark@easywaymanchester.co.uk
Website: www.allencarr.com

Leeds
Tel: 0800 077 6187
Therapist: Mark Keen
Email: mark@easywaymanchester.co.uk
Website: www.allencarr.com

Leicester
Tel: 0800 321 3007
Therapist: Rob Fielding
Email: info@easywaymidlands.co.uk
Website: www.allencarr.com

Lincoln
Tel: 0800 321 3007
Therapist: Rob Fielding
Email: info@easywaymidlands.co.uk
Website: www.allencarr.com

Liverpool
Tel: 0800 077 6187
Therapist: Mark Keen
Email: mark@easywaymanchester.co.uk
Website: www.allencarr.com

Manchester
Tel: 0800 077 6187
Therapist: Mark Keen
Email: mark@easywaymanchester.co.uk
Website: www.allencarr.com

Manchester—alcohol sessions
Tel: +44 (0)7936 712942
Therapist: Mike Connolly
Email: info@stopdrinkingnorth.co.uk
Website: www.allencarr.com

Milton Keynes
Tel: 0800 389 2115
Therapists: John Dicey, Colleen Dwyer,
Crispin Hay, Emma Hudson, Rob
Fielding, Sam Kelser, Rob Groves
Email: mail@allencarr.com
Website: www.allencarr.com

Newcastle/North East
Tel: 0800 077 6187
Therapist: Mark Keen
Email: mark@easywaymanchester.co.uk
Website: www.allencarr.com

Northern Ireland/Belfast
Tel: 0800 077 6187
Therapist: Mark Keen
Email: mark@easywaymanchester.co.uk
Website: www.allencarr.com

Nottingham
Tel: 0800 389 2115
Therapist: John Dicey, Colleen Dwyer,
Crispin Hay, Emma Hudson, Rob
Fielding, Sam Kelser, Rob Groves
Email: mail@allencarr.com
Website: www.allencarr.com

Reading
Tel: 0800 389 2115
Therapists: John Dicey, Colleen Dwyer,
Crispin Hay, Emma Hudson, Rob
Fielding, Sam Kelser, Rob Groves
Email: mail@allencarr.com
Website: www.allencarr.com

SCOTLAND
Glasgow and Edinburgh
Tel: +44 (0)131 449 7858
Therapists: Paul Melvin and Jim
McCreadie
Email: info@easywayscotland.co.uk
Website: www.allencarr.com

Southampton
Tel: 0800 389 2115
Therapists: John Dicey, Colleen Dwyer,
Crispin Hay, Emma Hudson, Rob
Fielding, Sam Kelser, Rob Groves
Email: mail@allencarr.com
Website: www.allencarr.com

Southport
Tel: 0800 077 6187
Therapist: Mark Keen
Email: mark@easywaymanchester.co.uk
Website: www.allencarr.com

Staines/Heathrow
Tel: 0800 389 2115
Therapists: John Dicey, Colleen Dwyer,
Crispin Hay, Emma Hudson, Rob
Fielding, Sam Kelser, Rob Groves
Email: mail@allencarr.com
Website: www.allencarr.com

Stevenage
Tel: 0800 389 2115
Therapists: John Dicey, Colleen Dwyer,
Crispin Hay, Emma Hudson, Rob
Fielding, Sam Kelser, Rob Groves
Email: mail@allencarr.com
Website: www.allencarr.com

Stoke
Tel: 0800 389 2115
Therapist: John Dicey, Colleen Dwyer,
Crispin Hay, Emma Hudson, Rob
Fielding, Sam Kelser, Rob Groves
Email: mail@allencarr.com
Website: www.allencarr.com

Surrey
Park House, 14 Pepys Road,
Raynes Park, London SW20 8NH
Tel: +44 (0)20 8944 7761
Fax: +44 (0)20 8944 8619
Therapists: John Dicey, Colleen
Dwyer, Crispin Hay, Emma Hudson,
Rob Fielding, Sam Kelser, Rob Groves,
Sam Cleary
Email: mail@allencarr.com
Website: www.allencarr.com

Watford
Tel: 0800 389 2115
Therapists: John Dicey, Colleen Dwyer,
Crispin Hay, Emma Hudson, Rob
Fielding, Sam Kelser, Rob Groves
Email: mail@allencarr.com
Website: www.allencarr.com

Worcester
Tel: 0800 321 3007
Therapist: Rob Fielding
Email: info@easywaymidlands.co.uk
Website: www.allencarr.com

WORLDWIDE CENTRES

REPUBLIC OF IRELAND
Dublin and Cork
Lo-Call (From ROI)
1 890 ESYWAY (37 99 29)
Tel: +353 (0)1 499 9010 (4 lines)
Therapists: Brenda Sweeney and Team
Email: info@allencarr.ie
Website: www.allencarr.com

AUSTRALIA
ACT, NSW, NT, QSL, VIC
Tel: 1300 848 028
Therapist: Natalie Clays
Email: natalie@allencarr.com.au
Website: www.allencarr.com

South Australia
Tel: 1300 848 028
Therapist: Jaime Reed
Email: sa@allencarr.com.au
Website: www.allencarr.com

Western Australia
Tel: 1300 848 0281
Therapist: Dianne Fisher
Email: wa@allencarr.com.au
Website: www.allencarr.com

AUSTRIA
Sessions held throughout Austria
Freephone: 0800RAUCHEN
(0800 7282436)
Tel: +43 (0)3512 44755
Therapists: Erich Kellermann and Team
Email: info@allen-carr.at
Website: www.allencarr.com

BAHRAIN—opening 2018
Website: www.allencarr.com

BELGIUM
Antwerp
Tel: +32 (0)3 281 6255
Fax: +32 (0)3 744 0608
Therapist: Dirk Nielandt
Email: info@allencarr.be
Website: www.allencarr.com

BRAZIL
São Paulo
Therapists: Alberto Steinberg &
Lilian Brunstein
Email: contato@easywaysp.com.br
Tel Lilian - (55) (11)99456-0153
Tel Alberto - (55) (11)99325-6514
Website: www.allencarr.com

BULGARIA
Tel: 0800 14104 / +359 899 88 99 07
Therapist: Rumyana Kostadinova
Email: rk@nepushaveche.com
Website: www.allencarr.com

CANADA
Sessions held throughout Canada
Toll free: +1-866 666 4299 /
+1 905 849 7736
English Therapist: Damian O'Hara
French Therapist: Rejean Belanger
Email: info@theeasywaytostopsmoking.com
Website: www.allencarr.com

CHILE
Tel: +56 2 4744587
Therapist: Claudia Sarmiento
Email: contacto@allencarr.cl
Website: www.allencarr.com

CZECH REPUBLIC
Tel: +420 234 261 787
Therapist: Dagmar Janecková
Email: dagmar.janeckova@allencarr.cz
Website: www.allencarr.com

DENMARK
Sessions held throughout Denmark
Tel: +45 70267711
Therapist: Mette Fonss
Email: mette@easyway.dk
Website: www.allencarr.com

ESTONIA
Tel: +372 733 0044
Therapist: Henry Jakobson
Email: info@allencarr.ee
Website: www.allencarr.com

FINLAND
Tel: +358-(0)45 3544099
Therapist: Janne Ström
Email: info@allencarr.fi
Website: www.allencarr.com

FRANCE
Sessions held throughout France
Freephone: 0800 386387
Tel: +33 (4)91 33 54 55
Therapists: Erick Serre and Team
Email: info@allencarr.fr
Website: www.allencarr.com

GERMANY
Sessions held throughout Germany
Freephone: 08000RAUCHEN
(0800 07282436)
Tel: +49 (0) 8031 90190-0
Therapists: Erich Kellermann and Team
Email: info@allen-carr.de
Website: www.allencarr.com

GREECE
Sessions held throughout Greece
Tel: +30 210 5224087
Therapist: Panos Tzouras
Email: panos@allencarr.gr
Website: www.allencarr.com

GUATEMALA
Tel: +502 2362 0000
Therapist: Michelle Binford
Email: bienvenid@dejedefumarfacil.com
Website: www.allencarr.com

HONG KONG
Email: info@easywayhongkong.com
Website: www.allencarr.com

HUNGARY
Seminars in Budapest and 12 other cities
across Hungary
Tel: 06 80 624 426 (freephone) or
+36 20 580 9244
Therapist: Gabor Szasz
Email: szasz.gabor@allencarr.hu
Website: www.allencarr.com

ICELAND
Reykjavik
Tel: +354 588 7060
Therapist: Petur Einarsson
Email: easyway@easyway.is
Website: www.allencarr.com

INDIA
Bangalore and Chennai
Tel: +91 (0)80 4154 0624
Therapist: Suresh Shottam
Email: info@easywaytostopsmoking.co.in
Website: www.allencarr.com

IRAN—opening 2018
Tehran and Mashhad
Website: www.allencarr.com

ISRAEL
Sessions held throughout Israel
Tel: +972 (0)3 6212525
Therapists: Ramy Romanovsky,
Orit Rozen
Email: info@allencarr.co.il
Website: www.allencarr.com

ITALY
Sessions held throughout Italy
Tel/Fax: +39 (0)2 7060 2438
Therapists: Francesca Cesati and Team
Email: info@easywayitalia.com
Website: www.allencarr.com

JAPAN
Sessions held throughout Japan
www.allencarr.com

LEBANON
Tel: +961 1 791 5565
Therapist: Sadek El-Assaad
Email: stopsmoking@allencarreasyway.me
Website: www.allencarr.com

MAURITIUS
Tel: +230 5727 5103
Therapist: Heidi Hoareau
Email: info@allencarr.mu
Website: www.allencarr.com

MEXICO
Sessions held throughout Mexico
Tel: +52 55 2623 0631
Therapists: Jorge Davo
Email: info@allencarr-mexico.com
Website: www.allencarr.com

NETHERLANDS
Sessions held throughout the Netherlands
Allen Carr's Easyway 'stoppen met roken'
Tel: (+31)53 478 43 62 /
(+31)900 786 77 37
Email: info@allencarr.nl
Website: www.allencarr.com

NEW ZEALAND
North Island – Auckland
Tel: +64 (0)27 4139 381
Therapist: Vickie Macrae
Email: vickie@easywaynz.co.nz
Website: www.allencarr.com

South Island – Dunedin and Invercargill
Tel: +64 (0)27 4139 381
Therapist: Debbie Kinder
Email: easywaysouth@icloud.com
Website: www.allencarr.com

NORWAY
Oslo
Tel: +47 93 20 09 11
Therapist: René Adde
Email: post@easyway-norge.no
Website: www.allencarr.com

PERU
Lima
Tel: +511 637 7310
Therapist: Luis Loranca
Email: lloranca@dejardefumaraltoque.com
Website: www.allencarr.com

POLAND
Sessions held throughout Poland
Tel: +48 (0)22 621 36 11
Therapist: Anna Kabat
Email: info@allen-carr.pl
Website: www.allencarr.com

PORTUGAL
Oporto
Tel: +351 22 9958698
Therapist: Ria Slof
Email: info@comodeixardefumar.com
Website: www.allencarr.com

ROMANIA
Tel: +40 (0)7321 3 8383
Therapist: Diana Vasiliu
Email: raspunsuri@allencarr.ro
Website: www.allencarr.com

RUSSIA
Moscow
Tel: +7 495 644 64 26
Therapist: Alexander Fomin
Email: info@allencarr.ru
Website: www.allencarr.com

St Petersburg
Website: www.allencarr.com

SAUDI ARABIA—opening 2018
Website: www.allencarr.com

SERBIA
Belgrade
Tel: +381 (0)11 308 8686
Email: office@allencarr.co.rs
Website: www.allencarr.com

SINGAPORE
Tel: +65 62241450
Therapist: Pam Oei
Email: pam@allencarr.com.sg
Website: www.allencarr.com

SLOVAKIA
Tel: +421 233 04 69 92
Therapist: Peter Sánta
Email: peter.santa@allencarr.sk
Website: www.allencarr.com

SLOVENIA
Tel: 00386 (0)40 77 61 77
Therapist: Gregor Server
Email: easyway@easyway.si
Website: www.allencarr.com

SOUTH AFRICA
Sessions held throughout South Africa
National Booking Line: 0861 100 200
Head Office: 15 Draper Square,
Draper St, Claremont 7708, Cape Town
Cape Town: Dr Charles Nel
Tel: +27 (0)21 851 5883
Mobile: 083 600 5555
Therapists: Dr Charles Nel, Malcolm
Robinson and Team
Email: easyway@allencarr.co.za
Website: www.allencarr.com

SOUTH KOREA
Seoul
Tel: +82 (0)70 4227 1862
Therapist: Yousung Cha
Email: master@allencarr.co.kr
Website: www.allencarr.com

SWEDEN
Tel: +46 70 695 6850
Therapists: Nina Ljungqvist,
Renée Johansson
Email: info@easyway.se
Website: www.allencarr.com

SWITZERLAND
Sessions held throughout Switzerland
Freephone: 0800RAUCHEN
(0800/728 2436)
Tel: +41 (0)52 383 3773
Fax: +41 (0)52 3833774
Therapists: Cyrill Argast and Team
For sessions in Suisse Romand and
Svizzera Italiana:
Tel: 0800 386 387
Email: info@allen-carr.ch
Website: www.allencarr.com

TURKEY
Sessions held throughout Turkey
Tel: +90 212 358 5307
Therapist: Emre Ustunucar
Email: info@allencarrturkiye.com
Website: www.allencarr.com

UNITED ARAB EMIRATES
Dubai and Abu Dhabi
Tel: +971 56 693 4000
Therapist: Sadek El-Assaad
Email: iwanttoquit@allencarreasyway.me
Website: www.allencarr.com

OTHER ALLEN CARR PUBLICATIONS

Allen Carr's revolutionary Easyway method is available in a wide variety of formats, including digitally as audiobooks and ebooks, and has been successfully applied to a broad range of subjects.

For more information about Easyway publications, please visit **shop.allencarr.com**

Stop Smoking Now/(US) Allen Carr's Quit Smoking without Willpower

Stop Smoking with Allen Carr (with 70-minute audio CD)

Your Personal Stop Smoking Plan

The Illustrated Easy Way to Stop Smoking

Finally Free!

Smoking Sucks (Parent Guide with 16 page pull-out comic)

The Little Book of Quitting

The Illustrated Easy Way to Stop Smoking

The Easy Way for Women to Stop Smoking/(US) Allen Carr's Easy Way for Women to Quit Smoking

How to Be a Happy Non-Smoker

No More Ashtrays

Smoking Sucks (Parent Guide with 16 page pull-out comic)

The Only Way to Stop Smoking Permanently

How to be a Happy Non-Smoker

Stop Smoking and Quit E-cigarettes

How to Stop Your Child Smoking

The Easy Way to Control Alcohol

Stop Drinking Now/(US) Allen Carr's Quit Drinking without Willpower

Your Personal Stop Drinking Plan

The Easy Way for Women to Stop Drinking/(US) Allen Carr's Easy Way for Women to Quit Drinking

The Illustrated Easy Way to Stop Drinking

No More Hangovers

The Easy Way to Mindfulness

Good Sugar Bad Sugar

The Easy Way to Quit Sugar

Lose Weight Now

The Easy Way for Women to Lose Weight/(US) Allen Carr's Easy Way for Women to Lose Weight

No More Diets

The Easy Way to Stop Gambling

No More Gambling

No More Worrying

Get Out of Debt Now

No More Debt

The Easy Way to Enjoy Flying

No More Fear of Flying

The Easy Way to Quit Coffee

Burning Ambition

Packing It In The Easy Way (the autobiography)

Want Easyway on your **smartphone** or **tablet**?
Search for "Allen Carr" in your app store.

Easyway publications are also available as **audiobooks**.
Visit **shop.allencarr.com** to find out more.

DISCOUNT VOUCHER
for
ALLEN CARR'S
EASYWAY CENTRES

Recover the price of this book when you attend an
Allen Carr's Easyway Centre
anywhere in the world!

Allen Carr's Easyway has a global network of stop
smoking centres where we guarantee you'll find it easy
to stop smoking or your money back.

**The success rate based on this
unique money-back guarantee is over 90%.**

Sessions addressing weight, alcohol and other
drug addictions are also available at certain centres.

When you book your session, mention this
voucher and you'll receive a discount of
the price of this book. Contact your nearest
centre for more information on how the sessions
work and to book your appointment.

**Details of Allen Carr's Easyway
Centres can be found at
www.allencarr.com
or call 0800 389 2115**

This offer is not valid in conjunction with any other offer/promotion.